Navigating the
National Board
Certification
Process

CORWIN PRESS

The Corwin Press logo—a raven striding across an open book—represents the union of courage and learning. Corwin Press is committed to improving education for all learners by publishing books and other professional development resources for those serving the field of K–12 education. By providing practical, hands-on materials, Corwin Press continues to carry out the promise of its motto: **"Helping Educators Do Their Work Better."**

Navigating the National Board Certification Process

A Step-by-Step Workbook for Teachers

Martha H. Hopkins

CORWIN PRESS
A Sage Publications Company
Thousand Oaks, California

For information:

Corwin Press
A Sage Publications Company
2455 Teller Road
Thousand Oaks, California 91320
E-mail: order@corwinpress.com

Sage Publications Ltd.
1 Oliver's Yard
55 City Road
London, EC1Y 1SP
United Kingdom

Sage Publications India Pvt. Ltd.
B-42, Panchsheel Enclave
Post Box 4109
New Delhi 110 017 India

Printed in the United States of America

Library of Congress Cataloging-in-Publication Data

Hopkins, Martha H.
Navigating the National Board certification process : a step-by-step workbook for teachers/by Martha H. Hopkins.
     p. cm.
Includes bibliographical references and index.
  ISBN 0-7619-3135-X (cloth)—ISBN 0-7619-3136-8 (paper)
1. Teachers—Certification—United States—Handbooks, manuals, etc. 2. Education—Standards—United States—Handbooks, manuals, etc. 3. National Board for Professional Teaching Standards (U.S.)—Handbooks, manuals, etc. I. Title.
LB1771.H67 2004
379.1'57—dc22   2004004596

This book is printed on acid-free paper.

     06   07   08   09   10   9   8   7   6   5   4   3   2

Acquisitions Editor:	Rachel Livsey
Editorial Assistant:	Phyllis Cappello
Production Editors:	Kristen Gibson/Tracy Alpern
Copy Editor:	Mary Tederstrom
Proofreader:	Tricia Lawrence
Typesetter:	C&M Digitals (P) Ltd.
Indexer:	Teri Greenberg
Cover Designer:	Terry Taylor

Contents

Introduction

What is an accomplished teacher? When asked to describe the teachers who have made a difference in their lives, people often talk about teachers who were demanding, but fair, who would not accept substandard work, and who encouraged their students to do and learn things that they had previously thought were beyond their grasp. They remember teachers who showed interest in them as individuals, not merely as members of a class. And they often mention teachers who were interesting, well informed adults who were able to make their subjects come alive in the classroom.

Consider the teachers you've had over the years. How many of them possessed those qualities? Most of us are lucky to name a handful at best. Recognizing the need to improve the quality of America's schools, the National Board for Professional Teaching Standards (NBPTS) was formed in 1987, following publication of the Carnegie report *A Nation Prepared: Teachers for the 21st Century.* The purpose of the NBPTS was to establish high and rigorous standards for what accomplished teachers should know and be able to do; to develop and operate a national, voluntary system to assess and certify teachers who meet these standards; and to advance related education reforms for the purpose of improving student learning in American schools. In 1989, the NBPTS published its Five Core Propositions which, when taken together, define accomplished teaching and provide a structure and direction for systematic professional development. Since that time, committees comprised largely of teachers have written standards that describe in detail how the Five Core Propositions apply to each of the certificate areas, and, by 2003, nearly 24,000 teachers earned the credential of National Board Certified Teacher (NBCT). As teachers complete the required assessments they must look deeply into their practice and justify every instructional decision within the context of the standards for accomplished teaching in their particular area of certification. As a result, teachers who have experienced this process are aware of what teachers should know and be able to do and are able to make appropriate choices within that framework. But more importantly, students now have a better chance of experiencing teachers who are reflective, competent, knowledgeable, enthusiastic, and compassionate.

The word *rigorous* has been commonly used by candidates seeking National Board Certification, not just in reference to the standards, but as a description of the assessment process itself. Over the period of one calendar year, candidates document their practice in portfolio entries, and they demonstrate their content knowledge on a written examination. The process on any given day may be regarded as difficult, exhilarating, discouraging, time-consuming, or enlightening, but it is almost always powerful and revealing. Some candidates complete the process in isolation, whereas others work in groups. Some enter the process before they're professionally or emotionally ready; others enter with little or no understanding of the rigors of the process. Most candidates, no matter how prepared they think they are going into the process, look back after it's all over and say, "If only I'd known. . . ." This book is designed to address many of these issues.

While working on my National Board assessments, I enjoyed support from my colleagues, family, and friends, but I wished I had (a) been more adequately prepared for the process before my clock started ticking; (b) been guided through the process more systematically; and (c) been prepared for the emotional rollercoaster that accompanied the process, the waiting period between completion and scoring, and the period following certification. This book is designed to help teachers understand the components of accomplished teaching as defined by the NBPTS, determine their readiness to enter into the National Board Certification process, and provide them with the skills and tools needed to move through that process with confidence. It can be used by teachers when deciding if National Board Certification is for them; by candidates working alone or in groups; and by teachers, administrators, staff developers, and/or professors who provide support to teachers as they complete the National Board Certification journey.

ABOUT THE BOOK

Navigating National Board Certification is much like preparing for any journey. In order to ensure a safe and enjoyable trip, it is first important to assess your skills and resources in relation to the conditions of the place you wish to visit (e.g., do you have the skills necessary to bike the trails or swim in the waters, do you have the necessary equipment, etc.). Once you've determined that you possess the necessary skills and resources, it's important to plan your journey (the places you hope to visit, the provisions you'll need to bring, clothing you'll need to pack, maps required, etc.). Finally, your journey begins. No matter how much planning you've done ahead of time, however, situations inevitably arise for which you were unprepared (flat tire, late plane, unexpected storm). But your skills, creativity, and traveling companions help you navigate safely to your final destination. Upon your return home, you reflect on the entire experience and begin planning for your next journey.

This book has been designed to help you navigate the entire National Board Certification journey. Part I, Choosing Your Destination, will help you determine if National Board Certification is an appropriate destination for you. You will be introduced to the Five Core Propositions, the standards for your certification area, the portfolio, and the tests that assess your content knowledge. Throughout this section you will complete a number of charts that, taken together, will reveal the strengths and weaknesses of your practice and help you determine if you are ready to apply for National Board Certification.

Once you have determined that you have the skills necessary to pursue this goal, Part II, Packing Your Bags, will help you make all necessary arrangements for completing the requirements of the portfolio and the content knowledge assessment. In this section, you will plan the units of study you will later highlight in your portfolio, create a support system, schedule your time, and practice making videotapes.

Part III, Making the Journey, will assist you on the actual journey. In this section you will analyze student work, analyze your videotapes, refresh your writing skills, and make final preparations for the content area examinations.

When all components of the process are completed to your satisfaction, you'll submit your work to the National Board and begin the journey back home. In Part IV, Returning Home, you will reflect upon your journey, celebrate the fact that you completed it, and begin the process of choosing your next professional destination.

HOW TO USE THE BOOK

It is helpful to think of this book as a tour guide. Typically a tour book includes incredible amounts of information designed to make a trip more enjoyable: descriptions of locations, maps, charts, rules/regulations that are specific to the sites being visited, suggested routes, and general advice. Travelers may choose to read the book in its entirety prior to making the trip; they may read selected portions of the book while planning the journey and fine-tune their plans by referring to the guide throughout their trip; or they may choose to wait until they board the plane to begin reading any of the information provided.

Like most tour books, this volume includes a great deal of information about each leg of the National Board Certification journey. Travelers (teachers) who have very little knowledge of the NBPTS Five Core Propositions and Standards and who have little experience analyzing their own practice will want to begin their journey with page one, completing all of the activities slowly and thoughtfully. Teachers who enter the process with a working knowledge of the Core Propositions and Standards and those who are already candidates, however, may wish to browse the material in Part I, Chapter 1 (What Is Accomplished Teaching?) and proceed directly to Chapter 2 (Am I Ready for the Journey?). Because of the sequential nature of the material presented in each of the successive chapters, I highly recommend that candidates choose not to skip directly to Making the Journey. Although completion of the portfolio and the assessments is emphasized in Making the Journey, candidates will find the process much easier to navigate if they complete as many of the preliminary activities as possible.

NAVIGATING THE NBPTS WEB SITE

A great many resources are available on the NBPTS Web site (http://www.nbpts.org). Throughout this book, you will be directed to places on this site. Like most good Web sites, this one is constantly being updated and improved. It is quite likely, therefore, that the information you seek on the site may not be found in quite the same place as it was when this book was written. Once you find the required information, you may wish to bookmark the exact location. Doing so will save you a great deal of time as you progress through the National Board Certification journey.

LET'S GET STARTED!

Now it's time to begin what is sure to be the most incredible and rewarding journey of your professional life. Use the activities in this book to guide you through each leg of the National Board Certification journey. While doing so you will not only improve your chances of becoming certified, but you will most assuredly raise the level of your practice to heights that heretofore were unimaginable!

NOTE

Although representative of typical National Board experience, all situations, scenarios, and portfolio excerpts included in this book are fictitious.

Acknowledgments

I'd like to thank all of the accomplished teachers who have so openly shared their thoughts and debated educational issues with me over the years. It is through these rich conversations that knowledge of content, children, and self began to blend into a unified whole. I would like most particularly to thank the principal and teachers at Dommerich Elementary School for taking this college professor under their wing to refresh my knowledge of the field, renew my passion for teaching, and support me through the National Board Certification process.

Two very special teachers served as mentors, editors, critics, colleagues, and friends while this book was being written. Sandy Hayes (MC Gen) and Susie Teague (EC Gen) are perhaps the most accomplished teachers and treasured friends I know. Not only have I been enriched by their presence in my life, but the children whose lives they touch are changed forever.

I'd also like to thank Rachel Livsey and Phyllis Cappello at Corwin Press for their infinite patience through the process of writing several drafts of the manuscript; Sandy Robinson, Dean of the College of Education at the University of Central Florida, for supporting me when I requested a leave of absence to pursue National Board Certification; and Betty Castor, former president of the NBPTS, for encouraging me to remain involved with the National Board after returning to the university.

Finally, I want to thank my husband for his endless patience, love, understanding, support, and encouragement.

Marty Hopkins
Professor and MC Gen 99

Contributions from the following reviewers are gratefully acknowledged:

Davey McClay, NBCT
Teacher/Trainer
Los Angeles Unified School District
Van Nuys, CA

Adrienne Mack-Kirschner, NBCT
Education Consultant
Los Angeles, CA

About the Author

 **Martha H. Hopkins** (Marty) is Professor of Education at the University of Central Florida. Before joining the university Marty taught Grades 2, 3, 4, and 5 in public and private schools in New Jersey and Florida and coordinated a Title I Math program in Ocala, Florida. She received her Masters of Education degree at the University of Florida and her PhD at The Florida State University. After teaching at UCF for 15 years, she became concerned that the methods and materials she was teaching in her undergraduate classes might be out of date. At the same time, the university began to discuss National Board Certification and the implications it would have on its graduate and undergraduate programs. Marty requested permission to return to the elementary classroom for one year to refresh her teaching skills and to apply for National Board Certification.

Since returning to the university Marty has immersed herself in National Board initiatives. She teaches several online candidate-support classes, hosts a conference for Florida NBCTs each spring, and is presently creating a teacher leadership degree for teachers who want to expand their leadership role while staying in the classroom.

Marty and her husband live in Florida. They are avid sailors and enjoy traveling through the wine country of California.

List of NBPTS Acronyms

EC Gen	Early Childhood Generalist
MC Gen	Middle Childhood Generalist
EA Gen	Early Adolescence Generalist
EMC Art	Early and Middle Childhood Art
EAYA Art	Early Adolescence through Young Adulthood Art
EAYA CTE	Early Adolescence through Young Adulthood Career and Technical Education
EMC ENL	Early and Middle Childhood English as a New Language
EAYA ENL	Early Adolescence through Young Adulthood English as a New Language
EA ELA	Early Adolescence English Language Arts
AYA ELA	Adolescence through Young Adulthood English Language Arts
ECYA ENS	Early Childhood through Young Adulthood Exceptional Needs
ECYA LM	Early Childhood through Young Adulthood Library Media
EA Math	Early Adolescence Mathematics
AYA Math	Adolescence through Young Adulthood Mathematics
EMC Music	Early and Middle Childhood Music
EAYA Music	Early Adolescence through Young Adulthood Music
EMC PE	Early and Middle Childhood Physical Education
EAYA PE	Early Adolescence through Young Adulthood Physical Education
ECYA SC	Early Childhood through Young Adulthood School Counseling
EA Sci	Early Adolescence Science
AYA Sci	Adolescence through Young Adulthood Science
EA SSH	Early Adolescence Social Studies History
AYA SSH	Adolescence through Young Adulthood Social Studies History
EAYA WLOE	Early Adolescence through Young Adulthood World Languages Other than English

Part I

Choosing Your Destination

National Board Certification is an incredible journey. Teachers who have made informed decisions to enter the process have almost universally indicated that although the process wasn't an easy one, it was one of the most rewarding professional experiences of their lives. No matter how accomplished they thought they were going into the process, almost all of them talk about how they grew as teachers while journeying through it. Is the National Board Certification credential an appropriate destination for you at this time?

Whenever considering a new destination it is always a good idea to collect as much information as possible about that destination as well as the requirements of the journey leading to it. Once you have collected all of the facts and compared them to your personal expertise and circumstance, you will be in a position to make an informed decision.

Information in this part of the book is designed to help you gather information about accomplished teaching as defined by the National Board for Professional Teaching Standards, the requirements of the journey toward National Board Certification, and the extent to which you feel ready to embark on that journey. If at the conclusion of these activities you make an informed choice to apply for National Board Certification, it's likely that your journey will be satisfying and the destination attainable.

What Is Accomplished Teaching?

The National Board for Professional Teaching Standards (NBPTS) seeks to improve the quality of education in America by establishing rigorous standards for accomplished teaching and certifying teachers who meet those standards. Before applying for certification from the NBPTS it is important to learn as much as possible about the standards they have established and to assess your practice against them.

There are Five Core Propositions that provide the framework for all NBPTS activities and assessments:

1. Teachers are committed to students and their learning.

2. Teachers know the subjects they teach and how to teach those subjects to students.

3. Teachers are responsible for managing and monitoring student learning.

4. Teachers think systematically about their practice and learn from experience.

5. Teachers are members of learning communities.

These Five Core Propositions were used to write a set of standards that define accomplished teaching for each certification area. So, although the title of the organization implies a single set of standards, there are as many sets of standards as there are certification areas (i.e., the standards for middle school English teachers are different from those for high school math teachers or fifth-grade teachers, etc.). All standards are based on the Five Core Propositions but differ within the context of the age of the students and the subject area(s) being taught. In August 2003, there were 24 different certificates and therefore 24 different sets of standards.

In this chapter you will read and study the core propositions and the standards for your certification area, identify teacher behaviors that demonstrate each of them, and assess your own practice in relationship to them.

CORE PROPOSITION 1: TEACHERS ARE COMMITTED TO STUDENTS AND THEIR LEARNING

What does it mean to be committed to your students? What do you do as a teacher that shows your commitment to them? What (if anything) is the difference between commitment to your students and commitment to their learning? Following are excerpts from conversations with teachers about their classrooms. Each of these conversations demonstrates commitment to students and their learning.

1. In the past I have relied solely on written vocabulary tests when assessing student knowledge of French. I have come to realize that this form of assessment favors the visual learners and places students with other strengths (auditory, kinesthetic, etc.) at a distinct disadvantage. Consequently, I planned an activity where students were grouped according to their identified intelligence [as defined by Gardner]. Each group was asked to solve a problem related to the French culture in a manner best suited to them. Group projects were shared with the class in French. (French teacher)

In this conversation, the French teacher reveals how she accomplishes the following:

- Provides multiple contexts in order to promote learning and evaluation
- Recognizes, respects, and accommodates individual differences
- Learns from previous experiences and alters plans accordingly
- Deeply roots instruction within learning theories

2. I was really surprised at the number of key signature mistakes that both girls made during the challenge. Both girls have been under quite an emotional strain from their home circumstances and showed signs of being embarrassed, so I did not want to pursue their evaluation in front of the class as I normally would. (Music teacher)

This music teacher demonstrates how he accomplishes the following:

- Knows students
- Recognizes that all instruction is diagnostic and adapts as necessary within a lesson

- Respects dignity and worth of each student
- Is attentive to variability of students

3. This group of students has a difficult time with honesty, anger management, and impulse control. The social expectations that have been developing within this group are to learn to identify a problem and work it out without reacting with anger and dishonesty. These issues continue to be a barrier for Mark and have increased since the family has become more unstable. (Exceptional Education teacher)

This exceptional education teacher demonstrates the following:

- Teaches individuals within group settings
- Emphasizes self-concept, social dynamics, civic virtues, and character development
- Knows students

4. I use a wide variety of curriculum and resources for continuous assessment, instruction, and remediation along with a very structured behavior management plan when working with Suzette. The social skills curriculum is integrated with the art curriculum and addresses the following areas: respect, conflict resolution, anger management, friendship, and trust. (Art teacher)

This art teacher demonstrates the following:

- Extends mission beyond cognitive capacity
- Respects diversity within group
- Teaches individuals in a group setting

Now that you have some knowledge of Core Proposition 1, it's time to read it in its entirety. To find it, please visit the NBPTS Web site: http://www.nbpts.org/about/index.cfm. Click on the phrase "Five Core Propositions" and you will find complete descriptions of the propositions in a format that can be copied into a word-processing document or downloaded as a PDF file. After studying the full description of the proposition, read the following scenario, noting evidence of Core Proposition 1.

Finding Evidence of Core Proposition 1

In the following scenario, a tenth-grade general math teacher is describing her approach to teaching statistics to a class of poorly motivated students. As you read the scenario, look for evidence of her commitment to her students and to their learning. As you find evidence, note it on the chart on the next page. The first section of the chart is done for you.

At the beginning of the year I administered an interest inventory, a learning style inventory, and an attitude survey. Results showed that an overwhelming majority of the students enjoy sports and video games, are visual and tactile learners, and have little idea of the use of mathematics in their world. Our city supports a professional football team. Capitalizing on the students' interests, I met with representatives from the team and, together, we mapped out a plan of study. The class was given passes to attend the first home game of the season. After the game, students followed the progress of one player on the team, calculating averages, graphing yardage or points, and the like while the class as a whole followed the progress of the team in relation to other teams in the league. I ordered a subscription to the local newspaper so we could compare our data with the "official" data reported after each game.

All of the students embraced this unit except Sally, a shy girl who recently moved to the area and expressed no interest in sports. I asked her to help me organize the unit—keeping tabs on which players the students were following, checking to be sure their calculations were correct, organizing displays of the class data, and so on. Completing each of these tasks allowed her the opportunity to learn the material without having to be immersed in the sports themselves.

Assessment for this unit took many forms. Realizing that traditional tests would most likely cause the students to revert to their negative attitude toward math, I assessed student progress as they presented their statistics after each game, I presented them with "story problems" containing fictitious data in small group settings where they could solve the problems together, and I noted their responses to questions raised in class discussions. Of course, it's also important that students understand statistics in contexts other than sports, so we researched and analyzed other incidences of statistics and graphs we found in the newspaper and on the Internet.

Chart 1.1   Core Proposition 1: Teachers Are Committed to Students and Their Learning

Core Proposition 1 Evidence	Is It There?	If So, Where?
Knows students	Yes	Based instruction on results of surveys; adjustment for Sally; alternative assessment
Alters/adapts to students while teaching		
Deepens knowledge of students based in recognized learning theories		
Capitalizes on strengths to nurture weaknesses		
Provides multiple contexts when evaluating learning (not just tests)		
Is attuned to and capitalizes on diversity		
Recognizes that there are no favorites or throwaway children (all equal attention)		
Does not treat all students the same		
Is concerned with student characteristics		
Develops student character		
Develops student civic responsibility		

Notes to Yourself:

_____

_____

_____

_____

CORE PROPOSITION 2: TEACHERS KNOW THEIR SUBJECTS AND HOW TO TEACH THEM TO STUDENTS

How does a teacher demonstrate knowledge of content? Is it in the *things* that are taught, the *way* things are taught, or perhaps a combination of the two? What's the difference between knowledge of content and knowledge of the discipline? Is it possible to have one without the other? Is one more critical in the classroom than the other?

Core Proposition 2 defines content knowledge, pedagogical content knowledge, and disciplinary thinking and describes teaching behaviors that indicate mastery of each. Following are excerpts from conversations with teachers about their classrooms. Each of these conversations demonstrates the teacher's mastery of content.

1. There has been a great deal of discussion among students and parents about the appropriateness of including the Harry Potter books in our school library. After debating the issue in class, the sixth-grade students hosted a public forum for the entire school community. Students from each side of the issue presented their arguments, and then they fielded questions from the audience. (Media Specialist)

In this conversation, the media specialist reveals how he accomplished the following:

- Develops critical thinking skills within discipline
- Applies content to real-world issues

2. After completing a simple one-day experiment with fresh cranberries, one of the students asked if the freshness of the berry would affect the results. Spurred on by this question other students began to ask questions—would the temperature of the berries change results? Would berry size make a difference? Capitalizing on this enthusiasm, I put aside my plans for the rest of the week and encouraged the students to create experiments dealing with variables of their choice. As a result, we didn't get as far through the written curriculum as other classes, but the students learned a great deal about the work of scientists! (Middle school Science teacher)

This science teacher shows evidence of Core Proposition 2 when she does the following:

- Extends teaching beyond facts to the way knowledge in the field is created
- Encourages critical thinking

- Helps students pose (and solve) problems
- Solves problems new to both students and teacher
- Recognizes that learning takes time

3. My class has been studying a variety of techniques to use when dealing with the public. The textbook contains many rich examples and nonexamples of conversations with customers. After reading and discussing these conversations, it became obvious to me that the students needed more hands-on experience in order to truly master the techniques. With the principal's blessing, teams of students created a product (employee relations) that was then sold to other students (customers) in the school store. (Career and Technical Education teacher)

This career and technical education teacher demonstrates the following:

- Provides practical application of content
- Employs methods most appropriate to content
- Employs multiple paths to knowledge

Now that you have some knowledge of Core Proposition 2, it's time to read it in its entirety. After studying the full description of the proposition, read the following scenario, noting evidence of Core Proposition 2.

Finding Evidence of Core Proposition 2

In the following scenario, a fifth-grade teacher is describing a portion of her science unit on the concept of matter. As you read the scenario, look for evidence of the components of Core Proposition 2. Note any evidence you find in the chart on the next page.

The objective of the lesson was for the students to develop their own working definition of matter. The children worked in small cooperative groups. Each person was assigned a role to encourage everyone's participation. I gave each small group a plastic bag full of items (wood blocks, sugar granules, soil, cotton balls, etc.). Other items/elements such as fire, air, heat, milk, and electricity were represented with words on index cards. I asked each group to make a chart using the headings "matter," "nonmatter," and "unsure." As the children began to work I moved from group to group asking questions that would encourage them to make careful observations, compare, and think about each item. At the end of the lesson, the speaker from each group shared their list of items that were the most difficult to classify. Some of the items that the children listed were air, water, steak, light, margarine, and fire. From the list, I realized that group definitions were not quite complete enough to distinguish matter from nonmatter. At the end of the lesson, I collected the children's journals in order to learn more about their thinking.

After reading my student's science journals and reflecting on the previous lesson, I realized that the children had some misconceptions about matter. Taking the concept further, I decided to conduct a class discussion and construct a class chart of all the definitions in order to reach a consensus. At the end of the discussion many students could say that matter "takes up space" and has "mass." However, they needed more time to test the items that appeared on their "unsure" list in order to build a more solid foundation for a more extended study of matter. Through questioning, I encouraged the children to think about how to conduct tests on items. Stations were set up with the materials necessary for the children to conduct their own tests (gram scales, paper bags, flashlights, balloons, etc.). As the children carried out their tests, I encouraged them to review their own definition of matter and make any necessary changes.

Chart 1.2   Core Proposition 2: Teachers Know Their Subjects and How to Teach Them to Students

Core Proposition 2 Evidence	Is It There?	If So, Where?
Understands role of disciplinary thinking		
Develops thinking skills within discipline(s)		
Encourages students to question recognized assumptions		
Demonstrates pedagogical content knowledge		
Combines knowledge of students and knowledge of content		
Encourages students to pose problems		
Uses multiple methods		
Develops nonlinear thinking		
Recognizes that learning cannot be rushed		

Notes to Yourself:

_____

_____

_____

_____

CORE PROPOSITION 3: TEACHERS ARE RESPONSIBLE FOR MANAGING AND MONITORING STUDENT LEARNING

Is there a difference between managing student behavior and managing student learning? How do teachers maximize learning opportunities for all students in their classes?

Core Proposition 3 details a variety of methods that accomplished teachers use to ensure student engagement and learning. Following are excerpts from conversations with teachers about their classrooms. Each of these conversations demonstrates some aspect of managing and monitoring student learning.

1. In preparation for student-led parent conferences, each of my students reviewed all work that had been collected throughout the semester. They were required to choose four products that best demonstrated their growth since the last grading period. They assessed their work against the standards we had agreed upon at the beginning of the term and wrote new objectives for the next grading period. Prior to the parent conference, all students met with me to share and/or revise their portfolios. (Fourth-grade teacher)

This fourth-grade teacher demonstrates the following:

- Involves students in self-assessment
- Uses portfolio assessment
- Provides constructive feedback

2. My general math class had just completed units of study relating to measurement, geometry, and ratio. Even though the book had mentioned practical applications of each topic, the students' lack of interest in these critical topics was staggering! I invited a local architect to visit the class to discuss the role of mathematics in her work. At the conclusion of the presentation, the students were literally sitting on the edge of their seats, begging for more. (Ninth-grade math teacher)

This ninth-grade math teacher demonstrates the following:

- Uses a variety of methods
- Uses outside resources
- Motivates by sparking new interests

3. There are a few students in this class who like to dominate discussions and have a hard time appreciating other points of view. In the past I have placed these students in the same group, but this time I chose to spread them out among the groups in an effort to help them develop

their discussion skills. I carefully placed them with students I knew would let them speak, but also would question and debate them if necessary. (Seventh-grade English teacher)

This English teacher demonstrates the following:

- Selects management techniques that encourage learning
- Meets individual student needs within a group setting
- Clearly articulates goals for individual students

4. Several students in this class have become much too dependent on their classmates and/or me when placed in problem-solving situations. For this reason, I required students to solve the area/perimeter problem individually and to record their solutions in their math journals. As they were working I roamed around the room, observing the problem-solving strategies of individual students and answering all questions by asking questions that would facilitate independent thinking. (Exceptional Education teacher)

This exceptional education teacher demonstrates the following:

- Assesses during activity
- Facilitates learning
- Monitors student engagement
- Focuses on learning, not behavior

Now that you have some knowledge of Core Proposition 3, it's time to read it in its entirety. After studying the full description of the proposition, read the following scenario, noting evidence of Core Proposition 3.

Finding Evidence of Core Proposition 3

In the following scenario, a sixth-grade teacher is describing a map lesson. As you read the scenario, look for evidence of the components of Core Proposition 3. Note any evidence you find in the chart on the next page.

I teach a class of 32 very bright sixth graders for 100 minutes at the end of the day. The students vary tremendously in learning style, but they are quite similar in their tendency to tune out of an activity after about 10 minutes.

I wanted the students to compare and contrast a variety of maps in order to see the relationship between the purpose of a map and the symbols used on it and to identify elements that maps have in common. We began the class as a whole group discussion in which we listed the kinds of maps they had used in the past. I then divided the class into groups of four and distributed a different kind of map (or maplike device) to each group (shaded relief, digital elevation, road, property survey, ski trail, navigation chart, landscape plan, and construction plan). Groups were given 5 minutes to study the map, determine its purpose, and note symbols and other characteristics of interest appearing on the map. I monitored each of the groups during this phase of the lesson not only to make sure that they understood the task but to ask guiding questions when necessary. I rang a bell at the conclusion of the 5 minutes and gave students 1 minute of silent time to add individual comments to their notes. Maps were then passed to the group to their right, and the process was repeated. In this manner, all students studied eight maps in about 50 minutes. We then came together as a class and charted similarities, differences, possible uses, and common elements of the eight maps.

I was intrigued with the excitement level of students during this lesson. The short duration of each task coupled with the variety of maps worked well to prevent off-task behaviors and boredom. More significantly, however, I noticed that the leadership roles in each group seemed to change depending on the map being studied. For example, the tactile learners assumed leadership when the shaded relief map was being studied; those with spatial strength particularly enjoyed the landscape plans; the logical-mathematical students thrived with the floor, property, and construction plans, and Sam, who is unusually difficult to motivate, transferred his interest in boating to assume a leadership role with the navigation chart.

Chart 1.3   Core Proposition 3: Teachers Are Responsible for Managing and Monitoring Student Learning

Core Proposition 3 Evidence	Is It There?	If So, Where?
Alters methods to meet student learning styles		
Varies setting		
Varies materials		
Uses human resources		
Varies group size		
Encourages independent thinking		
Organizes with a focus on learning, not behavior		
Motivates students		
Monitors student engagement		
Assesses constantly		
Recognizes that teachers teach individuals while managing groups		
Recognizes that individual students will learn different things from the same lesson		
Recognizes that assessment is not always grading		
Provides constant feedback		
Clearly articulates goals and all choices based on them		

Notes to Yourself:

_____

_____

_____

_____

CORE PROPOSITION 4: TEACHERS THINK SYSTEMATICALLY ABOUT THEIR PRACTICE AND LEARN FROM EXPERIENCE

Teachers have to make choices throughout each teaching day. Among other things, they must decide what should be taught, how it should be taught, and how to motivate each student. How does a teacher acquire the information necessary to make each of these decisions? Core Proposition 4 describes a variety of methods that accomplished teachers use to update their skills and knowledge in order to ensure that the decisions they make are the most appropriate for their students. Following are excerpts from conversations with teachers about their practice. Each of these conversations demonstrates some aspect of thinking systematically about their practice.

1. I love the new mathematics materials my school adopted this year! We are finally de-emphasizing rote calculation and concentrating instead on problem-solving approaches to mathematics. The parents are quite concerned and have requested that I ignore the new program. I feel certain that if parents understood the program, however, they would not be so displeased with it. Last night I hosted a math class for the parents. Although not all parents left the meeting totally convinced of the need to learn to think mathematically, they did begin to develop an appreciation for the new program. We agreed to continue holding "classes" throughout the year, and I agreed to watch the children carefully to make sure the new program doesn't have a negative effect on their readiness for middle school. (Fifth-grade teacher)

This fifth-grade teacher demonstrates the following:

- Justifies difficult choices
- Conducts classroom research

2. I've been toying with the idea of implementing literature circles in my advanced English Literature class for several years. Last month a colleague and I attended several sessions at the International Reading Association conference that provided us with wonderful ideas and resources. Since returning from the conference we have met almost every day and have designed a system that we think will work. We plan to begin the new approach next semester. (High school English teacher)

This high school English teacher demonstrates the following:

- Is a lifelong learner
- Uses current information to make thoughtful teaching choices

3. While working on my master's degree I became aware of the multiple intelligences research of Howard Gardner. At the time, I was working in a school located in a largely middle-class community. It was incredibly exciting to see the positive impact of altering my teaching methods to accommodate the learning styles of my students. I now work at a low performing school where the curriculum is largely scripted and I am frustrated that I can no longer vary my teaching methods. There must be a way! (First-grade teacher)

This first-grade teacher demonstrates the following:

- Is a lifelong learner
- Understands power of reflection
- Conducts classroom research

4. Last week Sam posed a problem that no one in the class could solve— and neither could I! At first I was hesitant to admit that I didn't know the answer, but then I realized that I had been given a wonderful opportunity to model learning with the students! We identified resources that could be used to help us, and we have been working together ever since. (Eleventh-grade Science teacher)

This science teacher demonstrates the following:

- Models critical thinking
- Models risk taking
- Is a lifelong learner

Finding Evidence of Core Proposition 4

In the following scenario, a kindergarten teacher is talking about how she has attempted to solve a dilemma in her classroom. As you read the scenario, look for evidence of the components of Core Proposition 4. Note any evidence you find in the chart on the next page.

Writing is an important part of my kindergarten curriculum. At the beginning of the school year most of the children tell their stories through pictures. Moving young children from the pictorial to the written word is a challenging responsibility. In October I was fortunate to attend a writing inservice that provided me with specific mini lessons I could use to improve student writing. After returning to the classroom, I couldn't wait to practice what I had learned, especially using a scoring rubric to assess the students' drawing and writing. It was the first tool I had ever seen to monitor and measure the growth of individual students and the class as a whole.

A month after attending the workshop and modeling the mini lessons I did not see the results I had hoped for. My students were still relying mostly on pictures and using few or no letters in their stories. They seemed to be spending a considerable amount of time off task during their writing time. The new scoring rubric confirmed that the children were not making the progress I had anticipated. Less than half of my class scored a Level 3 out of a score of 6. I wondered if the children needed more time and modeling or if the time they spent talking to each other was getting in the way of the writing progress.

I shared my concerns and work samples with a fellow teacher who attended the same writing inservice. I requested that she visit our classroom during writing time to observe the children and make notes about the conversations that were taking place as well as who was on and off task. I also asked her to score a class set of writing prompts using the rubric we were given in the workshop because I wanted someone impartial to score my student's writing. I was anxious to receive constructive feedback to find out more about my children and their writing.

The same teacher requested that I observe her writers workshop. After we had visited each others' classrooms we sat down and discussed what should come next in our writing programs.

Chart 1.4 Core Proposition 4: Teachers Think Systematically About Their Practice and Learn From Experience

Core Proposition 4 Evidence	Is It There?	If So, Where?
Is a lifelong learner		
Makes informed choices and justifiable compromises		
Seeks advice from colleagues		
Welcomes observations		
Understands power of reflection		
Stays current (professional development)		
Conducts classroom research		
Recognizes the significance of professional development		

Notes to Yourself:

_____

_____

_____

_____

CORE PROPOSITION 5: TEACHERS ARE MEMBERS OF LEARNING COMMUNITIES

Accomplished teachers interact with a wide variety of communities. They enjoy rich partnerships with parents and the local community, they participate in school and districtwide inservice activities, and they contribute significantly to professional organizations. Core Proposition 5 lists a variety of learning communities available to accomplished teachers and tells how involvement in them can significantly impact student learning. Following are excerpts from conversations with teachers about their practice. Each of these conversations demonstrates some aspect of their involvement with learning communities.

1. Realizing how important it is to integrate academics into my physical education curriculum, I chose to attend several mathematics workshops during our systemwide professional development day. Upon returning to the school, I met with each of the grade level teams in an effort to correlate my activities with their curriculum needs. (Elementary Physical Education teacher)

This physical education teacher demonstrates the following:

- Collaborates with colleagues
- Develops curriculum
- Shares expertise

2. In the past few weeks Sally has become quite withdrawn and seems to be losing a great deal of weight. Yesterday I arranged for Sally to visit with the school counselor. At the conclusion of the session, the counselor provided insight into Sally's problems and helped me plan future lessons for her. (Middle school Social Studies teacher)

This social studies teacher demonstrates the following:

- Identifies special needs students
- Collaborates with specialists

3. Last year I served on the school district textbook adoption committee. Rather than merely reading through the texts and making a decision, I chose to involve teachers in my school. I provided each team member with lessons from each of the texts. After teaching each lesson, we met as a team to discuss the appropriateness of the lesson for our students as well as the appropriateness of the content in general. I felt certain that my final vote on the committee represented the views of the entire team. (English as a New Language teacher)

This teacher demonstrates the following:

- Is a team player
- Coordinates instruction

4. I begin each year by making home visits. Meeting the students and parents/guardians in the comfort of their own homes helps to open lines of communication. At these meetings I share a bit about the curriculum and procedures of the class as well as information about myself, the students share a bit about themselves, and the parents discuss issues of concern they might have about the year. I also collect data at these visits in regard to how the parents/guardians might be able to contribute to the class throughout the year. As a result of these visits, students are more comfortable when they come to class on the first day, and a significant two-way communication system is begun with families. (Exceptional Education teacher)

This exceptional education teacher demonstrates the following:

- Engages parents and community

Finding Evidence of Core Proposition 5

In the following scenario, an elementary teacher is talking about a summer literacy program. As you read the scenario, look for evidence of the components of Core Proposition 5. Note any evidence you find in the chart on the next page.

The principal and teachers at our school were concerned that students were reading below grade level when they were being promoted to the next grade. As an elementary school teacher who has always had an interest in literacy development, I was eager to serve on a committee that would design a 4-week summer literacy program for teachers and students. This committee consisted of two classroom teachers, our curriculum resource teacher, and our school principal. We sought help outside of our school by inviting a literacy coach from our county administration office and a reading recovery teacher from a neighboring school to help us design our program.

It was decided that an important component of our program would be to include a teacher-coaching model. One to two teachers a week would join a classroom to observe, experience, and try new reading and writing strategies while teaching alongside the lead teacher. We hoped that this model would not only improve the literacy skills of the students attending summer school, but ultimately impact the entire school as a greater number of teachers became involved in the program.

The program we designed was implemented the following summer. The students who attended showed significant gains, but the highlight of each week may have been the reflection and discussion time the teachers shared after the students left every afternoon. This time was spent talking about what had occurred in the classroom and linking our experiences to the latest research in literacy development. The result of this reflection and discussion time was a deeper understanding through critical analysis of our teaching practices. We found that we were learning from each other.

Working together to plan and implement a summer school that would impact students and teachers led to a new form of collaboration. The following school year teachers across grade levels were continuing to discuss how new strategies were impacting their teaching and their students.

Chart 1.5 Core Proposition 5: Teachers Are Members of Learning Communities

Core Proposition 5 Evidence	Is It There?	If So, Where?
Collaborates with colleagues		
Is aware of and respectful of state and federal mandates		
Identifies special needs students and arranges for specialists to assist		
Is a team player		
Engages parents and community		

Notes to Yourself:

_____

_____

_____

_____

SUMMARY OF THE FIVE CORE PROPOSITIONS

The Five Core Propositions provide the framework for the entire National Board Certification journey. As generic competencies, they describe the state of the art for all teachers, no matter what subject or grade level they may teach. All accomplished teachers are committed to their students; are subject area experts; have a repertoire of effective teaching strategies; adapt methods and materials to the needs of individual students in their classes; motivate their students; intellectually engage their students in learning; constantly reflect on their practice, making changes as appropriate; involve parents and community in the learning of their students; and dedicate themselves to lifelong learning. When viewed individually, the Five Core Propositions may seem a bit overwhelming. Do *all* accomplished teachers, for instance, do *all* of the things listed in *each* proposition on any given day? Probably not.

Perhaps it is a good idea to consider the propositions in a broader context. As you studied them, you probably realized that, although there are five different propositions, there is quite a bit of overlap among them. That is to say, the activities of teaching may very well fall within more than one proposition, and some may fall into all five! Consider the teacher who invited the architect into her classroom. Was she

- providing multiple contexts to promote learning? (Core Proposition 1)
- using subject knowledge as an entrée into the real world? (Core Proposition 2)
- using human resources to motivate students? (Core Proposition 3)
- seeking the most current information about the subject? (Core Proposition 4)
- engaging the community? (Proposition 5)

When taken together, the propositions guide the daily work of all accomplished teachers. In the next few pages you will begin to reflect upon your own practice in relationship to these Five Core Propositions as applied to your specific certificate area.

THE STANDARDS

You have examined the Core Propositions, and now it is time to read the standards for your certification area. Each certificate area contains a set of approximately ten NBPTS standards that are based on the Five Core Propositions. The main difference between the two documents is the specificity of the standards. Whereas the core propositions define accomplished teaching across all grades and ages, the standards define accomplished teacher behaviors appropriate to the age of the students you teach and the content you present to them.

The standards provide the framework for describing your practice. They stress the importance of understanding the developmental age of the students you teach and the need to create environments that involve students in meaningful learning. They identify the strategies, methods, and practices that accomplished teachers use to teach diverse groups of students, and they emphasize the importance of developing collaborative partnerships with parents, colleagues, and the community.

The standards for each certification area are available for purchase and in PDF format on the NBPTS Web site (http://www.nbpts.org—Click on Candidate Resource Center, then, on the new page, click on Certificate Knowledge Center). You will need access to a copy of the standards for your certification area to complete the following activities. While you're visiting the Web site, you might also want to take a few minutes to read how the standards were developed.

Studying the Standards

It is impossible to overstate the importance of the standards for your certification area. Throughout the application process you will be asked to describe how your practice demonstrates each of the standards of accomplished teaching. One National Board Certified Teacher (NBCT) likes to tell people that she kept a copy of her standards under her pillow in hopes that the information would drift to her brain while she slept! The standards are fairly lengthy documents and can be difficult to read. However, they are well worth the effort. Studying them will help you define what good practice is and help you identify the elements in your own teaching that qualify you as an accomplished teacher.

The following activity provides you with a strategy for familiarizing yourself with each of the standards in your certification area. You will want to repeat this process with each of the standards, but please take your time. At the end of this exercise you should feel comfortable with the standards for accomplished teaching and have completed a pretty thorough self-assessment of your practice.

You will be reading each standard in your certificate area *three times*. As you read each standard, keep the following questions in mind:

- What would accomplished teachers do or say that demonstrates the standard in their practice?
- What proof is needed to show that a teacher meets this standard?

Procedures:

1. Read the entire standard straight through without taking notes. This will give you a broad overview of the content.

2. Reread the standard, noting things that you already do that demonstrate the standard in your practice. Many teachers prefer to jot notes directly in the margins of the standards document.

3. Read the standard one more time, noting those things that you don't presently include in your practice. Consider how you could include them.

Many teachers find it helpful to organize their thoughts about each standard in chart form. The following chart was completed by a high school science teacher.

As you can see, the teacher has realized that, although he already uses both formal and informal methods to assess his students, there are some areas that he could strengthen in order to meet the assessment standard for his certificate area. You will find a blank copy of the "Analyzing the Standards" form in Resource 1 of this book. Completing one chart for each of your standards will help you reflect on how they apply to your teaching.

Chart 1.6 Analyzing the Standards

Standard # _10_: _____ _Assessment_ _____
(Write the title of the standard here)

Evidence of This Standard in My Practice

Key Word or Phrase	What I Do	What I Could Do
Formal methods	Weekly exams	
Informal methods	Portfolios of lab work	Lab assessments; analyze thought processes while in lab
Ongoing	Portfolios	Observe daily to help direct future instruction
Beyond facts to processes	Portfolios	Analyze novel problem
Before instruction	Analyze content to be taught	?????
During instruction	Observe during labs; listen during group discussions	Ask facilitative questions while observing
After instruction	Factual exams	Write an essay; construct concept map
May be more than one day		Rethink use of exams as teaching tools
Student self-assessment		Have students select work to include in portfolio (maybe more than teacher assigned labs)

Is there anything in your practice that seems to be contrary to the standard (i.e., something that you might want to change)?

I seem to rely too heavily on formal assessment (exams); I need to turn more of the assessment over to the students—help them use science processes within assessments. I also need to find out what it means to assess _before_ instruction.

FREQUENTLY ASKED QUESTIONS

Must I do all of the things mentioned in the Core Propositions and the Standards in order to be considered an accomplished teacher?

No. The Five Core Propositions and the Standards for each certificate area describe the ideal teacher. Accomplished teachers constantly strive to meet the standard but often fall short. The key to accomplishment is self-awareness and persistent efforts to improve areas of weakness in order to ensure maximal student learning. That being said, it is important that candidates demonstrate accomplishment of most of the characteristics described in the two documents.

Suppose I'm weak in one area: Should I wait until I've improved my practice to begin the National Board process?

Not necessarily. Considered by many to be one of the most powerful staff development tools available today, the National Board's Five Core Propositions serve as the basis for preservice as well as inservice education throughout the country. It's important to note, too, that the NBPTS recognizes the professional development aspect of the process by allowing teachers 3 years to achieve certification (candidates must complete the entire process in the first year, but they may bank points and redo sections as desired over the following 2 years). As you reviewed your practice against the Five Core Propositions and Standards, if you found only a few weak areas in your teaching, you will most likely improve on them while completing the process. If you found many disagreements between your practice and the standards, you may wish to wait a while longer.

What if I don't agree that something in the standards is good teaching, or if it doesn't work with my students?

This is a very good question! Perhaps the answer lies in the number of disagreements you find between the standards and your own beliefs about teaching and learning. If you find many points of departure, the process could be a long and painful one for you. If you find only a few, you will most likely have no problems at all.

I teach in a low-performing school where the reading curriculum is scripted and I'm forbidden to vary from the text. There's no way I can show that I adjust methods and materials to the individual needs of my students. Should I forget all about National Board certification?

Not necessarily. Many elementary school teachers in your position have found ways to demonstrate their ability to adapt curriculum to the diverse needs of their students through use of integrated curriculum (i.e., teaching reading within the context of science). In the next chapter of this book you will be guided through the requirements of each portfolio entry. Keep the limitations of your situation in mind as you complete each of the tasks.

2

Am I Ready for the Journey?

Y ou will recall that the National Board for Professional Teaching Standards (NBPTS) has defined accomplished teaching in terms of what teachers know as well as what they do. To that end, when you apply for certification by the National Board you will be asked to complete a rather lengthy process involving a variety of assessments. You will be asked to describe, analyze, and reflect upon your classroom practice; to document your involvement with families and community; and to demonstrate mastery of the content you teach. Documentation of your classroom practice and involvement with families and community is generally done through a portfolio process. All candidates must complete several portfolio entries in which they might be asked to analyze student work, analyze videotapes of themselves teaching, or provide documentation of significant partnerships with families and communities. In addition, all candidates complete a written examination covering the content appropriate for their certificate area. When viewed as a whole, the assessment process seems overwhelming and more than just a little bit intimidating. When viewed as a set of separate components, however, the process becomes more manageable and even a bit enjoyable.

In this section you will assess your readiness to enter the process by familiarizing yourself with five components of the assessment process: (1) the writing skills you'll need to tell your story, (2) expectations of the portfolio entries, (3) content knowledge assessment, (4) work with families and community, and (5) time management. At the conclusion of these activities you should feel knowledgeable about the process and confident in your ability to complete it successfully.

WRITING REQUIREMENTS

As an accomplished teacher you no doubt spend a great deal of time writing. You write to your students, to their families, to your principal, and/or to your colleagues almost every day. If you're like most teachers, you're probably thinking that writing will be the very least of your worries while completing the National Board process. You may be surprised. It is usually not too long after candidates begin working on their entries that they realize how difficult it is to write clear, consistent, and convincing paragraphs.

Writing to people who know you about things they know about is much easier than writing to complete strangers who know nothing about you or about your teaching situation. The NBPTS assessors will know you only through your writing. It is incredibly important, therefore, that the words you choose paint a complete and accurate picture of both your practice and your passion for teaching.

There are three kinds of writing required in your National Board portfolio—description, analysis, and reflection. Even though they will seem to blend together in your writing, each of them is designed to answer a different set of questions about your teaching. When taken together, they provide the assessor a glimpse into your practice.

As you complete the writing activities that follow, you will very likely become much more sensitive to the words you write every day. Please try not to tune out those thoughts! The more you practice before starting your National Board assessments, the easier they will be for you to write.

Descriptive Writing

Descriptive writing illustrates, explains, delineates, and recounts. It is often helpful to think of it using words to paint a picture. Descriptive writing is called for in an entry when it asks you to state, list, or describe. Questions calling for description begin with what, which, who, when, where, or how (as in "How did you present the lesson?").

Entry prompts asking for description might look like the following:

- What are the relevant features of your teaching setting that influenced your selection of this prompt and these students?
- What activity immediately preceded the lesson featured on the videotape?
- Who is featured on the tape?
- What strategies did you use to ensure fairness, equity, and access?

The following charts contain examples and nonexamples of descriptive writing. As you compare and contrast the samples, you will note that descriptive writing tells, but makes no judgments or justifications.

Chart 2.1   Examples of Descriptive Writing

Writing Sample	Descriptive?	How Do You Know?
I provide the children with feedback during individual conferences and in group sharing times.	Yes	*Teacher is telling what she does to provide feedback to her students.*
Throughout the week children record their thoughts and feelings in journals, justify their answers and explain their thinking in learning logs, write personal and business letters as appropriate in various content areas, and write persuasive essays on a social or political issue.	Yes	*Teacher is telling what writing experiences his students have had.*
After Kay had identified sixths and twelfths as being part of the thirds family, I challenged the children to guess how many denominators represented in their set of fraction bars would be in the fifths family.	Yes	*Teacher is telling what occurred in the lesson featured on the videotape.*

Chart 2.2   Nonexamples of Descriptive Writing

Writing Sample	Descriptive?	How Do You Know?
Because the students in my classroom represent a wide range of achievement levels, backgrounds, and interests, I seldom assign a single writing prompt to the entire class during writers' workshop.	No	*Teacher is justifying his choice of strategies.*
I plan to make two important changes when teaching this content in the future. First, I plan to introduce the fraction bars at the very beginning of the unit. Introducing this linear model along with all of the others during the exploration phase will most likely deepen the children's understanding of fractions in general and will better prepare them for using the bars to add and subtract fractions later on.	No	*Tells what the teacher would do next time and how she thinks the changes will impact the students*
As we engaged in a rather heated debate about what the rules for the classroom should be, the seeds of compromise, sensitivity, and respect toward others were germinated.	No	*Teacher is making a judgment about the students' reactions. No specific evidence is provided.*

Is It Descriptive?

Following is a table containing several passages similar to those commonly found in National Board portfolios. Read each passage carefully. Refer to the previous pages to help you decide if the passage is descriptive. Support your answer in the third column. (Answers are provided at the end of this chapter.)

Chart 2.3 Is It Descriptive?

Writing Sample	Descriptive?	How Do You Know?
I have arranged the desks into groups of four so the students can engage in discussion frequently.		
Results of a learning styles inventory revealed that 80% of my students are auditory learners.		
Although Ms. Smith's classroom visit added a great deal of excitement, the students didn't appear to gain significant knowledge from her presentation.		
We played a game very similar to "Jeopardy" where the students were given an answer and were asked to generate an appropriate question for that response.		
William was retained in sixth grade because his work habits keep him from succeeding.		

Notes to Yourself:

_____

_____

_____

_____

Analytical Writing

The second kind of writing required in the National Board portfolio is analytical writing. It is by far the most difficult form of writing required and often makes the difference between achievement and nonachievement of National Board Certification. The National Board portfolio requires you to analyze both your students and yourself. Teachers often report that they are quite comfortable with analyzing students but equally uncomfortable with self-analysis.

Analytical writing critiques, justifies, provides rationale, shows thought processes that were used to arrive at conclusions, and interprets. It is called for when an entry asks why, in what ways, or how (as in "How do you know the lesson worked?"). When using analysis you are required to see beyond the facts, think deeply, interpret, connect, realize, question, and justify.

An entry prompt asking for analysis might look like the following:

- How do the individual student responses fit what you already know about this student's understanding, knowledge, and performance?
- How did your knowledge of the students' needs influence the planning and delivery of instruction?
- Why did you choose to use these materials?

The following charts contain examples and nonexamples of analytical writing. As you compare and contrast the samples, you will note that analytic writing is used to justify instructional choices and to make inferences about students and their learning.

Chart 2.4 Examples of Analytic Writing

Writing Sample	Analytical?	How Do You Know?
I chose to use multilink cubes for this lesson because they can be easily manipulated by the children, and they can be joined and separated in more than one direction.	Yes	*Teacher is justifying his choice of instructional materials.*
As I watched Lisa record Bryan's comment I could almost see her drawing a parallel between this comment and the reason her friend, Mary, sometimes bullies her.	Yes	*Teacher is making an inference about student learning. Facts are not presented.*
She can see things from his perspective, perhaps because it is similar to her own.	Yes	*Teacher is inferring why the student responded as she did.*

Chart 2.5   Nonexamples of Analytical Writing

Writing Sample	Analytical?	How Do You Know?
The students researched the plants and animals that live within our ecosystem, observed the area for evidence of plants that can survive on or near the grounds, collected data on rainfall in the area, and collected and analyzed soil samples on the site.	No	*Teacher is describing a set of activities.*
Next time I think I'll review and extend our previous activities before moving into something as sophisticated as this assignment.	No	*Teacher is looking to the future.*
Recently, Meg experienced death by cancer when one of her sister's best friends died at a very young age. She returned to school on Monday and immediately sat at the computer, wrote a poem titled "Cancer can't . . . ," and quietly placed it in her writing portfolio.	No	*Teacher is describing a student's actions.*

Is It Analytical?

Following is a table containing several passages similar to those commonly found in National Board portfolios. Read each passage carefully. Refer to the previous pages to help you decide if the passage is analytical. Support your answer in the third column. (Answers are provided at the end of this chapter.)

Chart 2.6   Is It Analytical?

Writing Sample	Analytical?	How Do You Know?
I have developed strong collaborative relationships with all of her therapists in order to design appropriate instructional strategies and realistic learning goals.		
I could feel them beginning to think about some of their favorite commercials a bit more critically.		
I introduced SQ3R by asking students what they thought the letters for this reading strategy stood for, starting with the 3R.		
In my future lessons, I will allow Sam more time to sound out the words before breaking them down for him.		
Her errors demonstrated lack of understanding in both French and English.		

Notes to Yourself:

_____

_____

_____

_____

Reflective Writing

The third (and final) kind of writing required in the National Board portfolio is reflective writing. Although it appears to be easier than analysis, it represents a blending of all three kinds of writing. As candidates reflect on their practice, they must consider the facts of the teaching episode (description) and the effects of those episodes on the students (analysis) in order to make judgments about future learning experiences for their students.

Reflective writing involves thinking seriously, contemplating, pondering, evaluating, and planning for the future based on the past. It is called for when an entry asks how successful the lesson was, what you would do differently, what changes you would make, what parts of the lesson you would keep the same, and why.

An entry prompt asking for reflection might look like the following:

- How successful was your use of writing as a way for students to explore and discover important ideas and understandings? What is your evidence?
- If you were given the opportunity to teach this particular sequence again with these students, what alternative strategies would you use? Why?

The following charts contain examples and nonexamples of reflective writing. As you compare and contrast the samples, you will see that description and analysis provide the background information for conclusions you make in the reflection portion of an entry. As you complete your own portfolio you'll use both description and analysis within your reflection as you tell what you would do differently (describe the new strategy) and how it would be more effective for your students (analysis).

Chart 2.7 Examples of Reflective Writing

Writing Sample	Reflective?	How Do You Know?
If given the opportunity to use these two writing prompts again I think I would use the expository prompt exactly as I did, but I would seriously reconsider the personification prompt. Although it seemed like a fun task, I think . . .	Yes	*Teacher is looking to the future and justifying the new choice.*
An important concept of systems is that some changes can be positive. During this study we constantly looked for negative impacts. It could have been more powerful if I had led the children to look for positive changes while seeking to avoid negative ones.	Yes	*Teacher is identifying a weakness and presenting a possibly more powerful alternative.*
I anticipate that the children and I will deal with each challenge openly, honestly, and respectfully in class meetings.	Yes	*Teacher is looking to the future.*

Chart 2.8   Nonexamples of Reflective Writing

Writing Sample	Reflective?	How Do You Know?
The three students in this cooperative group represent a wide range of academic and developmental levels.	No	*Teacher is describing the students.*
Students who entered into this activity having successfully completed all preliminary activities successfully achieved this goal.	No	*Teacher is describing student achievement.*
I felt certain after the conference that he understood the mathematics but was unsure about his commitment to do his own work.	No	*Teacher is making an inference about student learning. (analytical)*

Is It Reflective?

On the next page you will find a table containing several passages similar to those commonly found in National Board portfolios. Read each passage carefully. Refer to the previous pages to help you decide if the passage is reflective. Support your answer in the third column. (Answers are provided at the end of this chapter.)

Chart 2.9   Is It Reflective?

Writing Sample	Reflective?	How Do You Know?
I want them to begin to question what they read so that they can make informed decisions about what they read in and out of school.		
The biggest change I would make would be to allow for more time. The students rushed through the task and made many careless errors.		
The most meaningful form of feedback for me was teacher observation during the investigations, when I circulated to help students use the math materials.		
I ensure equity, fairness, and access for all students by including as many students as possible in discussion in this type of lesson.		
The fact that they were so engaged in the discussion, even as the bell rang, told me this was a topic they could relate to and enjoy learning more about.		

Notes to Yourself:

_____

_____

_____

_____

_____

_____

ASSESSING CLASSROOM PRACTICE

As you read and studied the Five Core Propositions and the Standards for your certificate area, you probably noticed that there is no single approach to teaching that is valued above all others. Accomplished teachers can be seen orchestrating small groups of students and they can just as easily be found lecturing to a class. The importance isn't what teachers do at any given time, but why they chose those methods and materials for those students at that time.

Obviously, the easiest way to assess classroom practice is to visit the classroom. Given the impracticality of that option when assessing teachers in all 50 states, the NBPTS has chosen to use portfolio assessment to determine the extent to which your teaching is compatible with the standards. Writing a portfolio entry is very much like telling a story to a given rubric. That is to say, you will be given the opportunity to tell your story by responding to a given set of questions specifically designed around the standards for your certificate area. Although the story is yours, the format is standardized.

Critical components of most classroom practice portfolio entries are videotapes of your teaching and/or examples of student work. Providing these artifacts allows the assessor to visit you and your students without having to travel. Later in this book you will be guided through the completion of your portfolio entries, your videotaping, and your analysis of student work. For now, it's important that you see what kinds of teaching and learning experiences you'll be asked to document in your entries.

Each candidate receives a box containing all information necessary to complete the portfolios as soon as their application has been fully processed. The NBPTS suggests, however, that all teachers who think they might want to seek certification become familiar with the process before making the commitment. For that reason complete portfolio directions for the current year are available on the NBPTS Web site (http://www.nbpts.org; click on Candidate Resource Center, then, on the next page, scroll down to Portfolio Instructions). Before reading further, visit the Web site and download the portfolio directions for your certificate.

As you browse through the directions you will notice that there is a great deal of useful information in the front sections of the booklet. In fact, much of the information can be used to supplement the activities you've completed thus far. Quite often candidates are so rushed to write their portfolios, they neglect to read this very critical information, making the entire process much more difficult than it has to be. Let's explore a small portion of the front matter.

Portfolio Expectations

Two portions of the directions booklet describe the kinds of portfolio entries you will be required to write: "Overview of the Entries" (which will probably start somewhere around page 4 of the portfolio directions booklet) and "Summary of the Portfolio Entries" (which probably starts somewhere near page 27). At this point you can ignore all reference to "Documented Accomplishments" because you'll work on that part separately. For now, please concentrate on entries dealing with classroom practice. Read these two sections very carefully to find out

- how many classroom practice entries there will be,
- what kinds of lessons you will need to discuss,
- if you will be asked to analyze student work,
- how many videotapes you will be required to submit,
- if there are any time restrictions on your instructional units,
- if there are restrictions regarding the students you may use,
- any other important information that you must remember.

Record all of the important information in the space below. You'll want to refer to this page frequently while planning your instruction during the year you apply for certification.

Notes to Yourself:

_____

_____

_____

_____

Evidence: Where's Your Proof?

The heart of the certification process is not telling your story, but rather providing evidence that your story reflects the standards and that what you say matches what you actually do in the classroom. Evidence is the "main ingredient" in the portfolio. It is the proof that you are "walking your talk." NBPTS will ask for evidence of standards such as those listed in Chart 2.10. After reviewing the chart carefully, complete the following:

1. Think about your teaching. Where could you find evidence of each standard? What would that evidence look like? Record your thoughts in the middle column of the chart.

2. Now videotape yourself teaching a lesson. Did you find evidence? What did it look like? Record your findings in the last column of the chart.

Chart 2.10 Evidence

Standard	Possible Evidence	Evidence on Tape
Demonstrates knowledge of students' backgrounds and skills		
Sets worthwhile goals		
Promotes students' active engagement and involvement in learning		
Assesses student learning		
Demonstrates knowledge of curriculum and/or content		
Provides a safe and inclusive learning environment		
Challenges students to think		
Meets the needs of diverse learners		
Uses appropriate teaching strategies		
Integrates curriculum to achieve student goals		
Plans lessons and units of study and links goals		
Engages students in meaningful interactions with teacher and peers		
Uses appropriate materials, resources, and technologies		

Following is an incomplete list of forms that evidence can take. How many of them can you find in your practice? Are there other forms of evidence not on this list?

Table 2.a   Form of Evidence

Student interviews	Home visits
Surveys	Self-assessments
Discussions	Brainstorming
Graphic organizers	Work samples
Tests	Performance assessments
Portfolios	Maps, charts, graphs
Discourse/dialogue	Journals
Classroom arrangement/design	Class meetings
Teacher demonstrations	Art project
Simulations	Explanations
Debates	Partner activities
Science experiments/Lab write-ups	Learning games
Learning material/equipment (microscopes, hand lenses, software, graphing calculators, math manipulative, videos, books, audiovisual equipment, digital cameras)	Grouping of students (small groups, pairs, cooperative groups) Projects (visual presentations, skits, plays, music, Power Point presentations, speeches)

Notes to Yourself:

_____

_____

_____

_____

KNOWLEDGE OF CONTENT

You will recall that the second Core Proposition states that teachers know the subjects they teach and how to teach those subjects to students. The portfolio addresses both parts of this proposition, but not fully. As you explored the types of activities and questions required in the portfolio, you no doubt realized that the emphasis in that part of the assessment is on how you teach content specific to your teaching assignment. For instance, if you are a high school algebra teacher, the Adolescence through Young Adulthood (AYA) Mathematics portfolio entries will help the reader assess your knowledge of algebra as demonstrated by the teaching and assessment strategies documented in your writing. However, an accomplished teacher as defined by the NBPTS is a person who possesses depth of knowledge in all content related to the area of certification being sought (i.e., all subjects a person with that certification might teach). To that end, a person seeking certification as an AYA Math teacher must demonstrate superior knowledge in all areas of mathematics included in the high school curriculum, not just algebra.

National Board Certification candidates are given the opportunity to demonstrate the depth of their knowledge by completing a computerized written examination. At the time of this writing, the exam is administered at specified learning centers located throughout the country and requires a maximum of 3 hours to complete. It is important to note, however, that the NBPTS is constantly updating its procedures, and it is quite possible that this exam will be available via home computer in the not-too-distant future. And of course the exam itself may change dramatically over time. Although the content included in the examinations varies greatly from certification to certification, the questions typically fall into two categories. Some questions will ask you to solve a problem in your subject area (analyze a poem, critique a piece of art, solve a math problem, etc.), whereas others will require you to apply your subject knowledge to a given scenario (identify a student's misconceptions, deal with a parent who wants a book removed from the library shelves, etc.). Items change from year to year but are always written from a publicized set of test specifications. The sooner you familiarize yourself with these specifications, the easier it will be for you to prepare for the assessment experience.

Let's begin by locating descriptions of items that are presently being used in your certification area. Once again we return to the NBPTS Web site. Realizing that the Web site is always being updated, the following information may not be current at the time you are reading this page. However, it will give you a good idea of the words and phrases that will be useful to you as you navigate the Web site.

Here's how to find descriptions of items:

1. Go to http://www.nbpts.org

2. Click on
   a. Candidate Resource Center
   b. 200x–200x Candidate Information (click on the year that represents current candidates)
   c. Certificate Knowledge Center
   d. "assessment center orientation" under your certificate area
   e. view exercise description

3. Find your certificate area in the pull-down menu.

Now you should have the descriptions of the items included on the most recent test. Please note that these are not specific questions. Instead they describe the kind of knowledge you will be asked to demonstrate, and they also tell you if each item is scenario based or strictly a test of your knowledge of content.

As you read each item description, make notes to yourself about the breadth of content tested as well as the kinds of items you encounter. Is there anything you feel a need to brush up on?

Notes to Yourself:

_____

_____

_____

_____

WORK WITH FAMILIES AND COMMUNITY

Accomplished teaching as defined by the NBPTS requires that teachers reach beyond their classroom to a variety of learning communities. Although it is possible to teach a group of students without developing partnerships with the students' families and/or the community, the NBPTS believes that it is highly unlikely that such practices will provide the most appropriate educational opportunities for all students. In fact, the work of teachers outside their classrooms is of such importance to the NBPTS that it is discussed in detail in two of the Five Core Propositions (4 and 5), and one of the portfolio entries is reserved exclusively for documentation of these accomplishments. In this portfolio entry, you will be asked to document

- your efforts to develop and sustain meaningful partnerships with students' families;
- your efforts to develop and sustain meaningful partnerships with the community;
- your contributions as a leader and a collaborator with other professionals within a variety of learning communities;
- your growth as a learner.

When documenting accomplishments, you will be analyzing neither student work nor a videotape of your practice. Instead you will describe and analyze activities you have done in the past 5 years (or during the current year, in the case of family partnerships) that address each of the components listed earlier. It is critical to note here that the word accomplishment has been well chosen. For purposes of the portfolio, a professional activity becomes an accomplishment only if it results in a significant (and identifiable) impact on student learning and it was not a requirement of your job. Holding a parent meeting on Back-to-School Night, for example, is probably not an accomplishment (it's required), but having the students create and film a videotape of the class routines to be presented during

Back-to-School Night might be. Serving as teacher of the year is most likely not an accomplishment in and of itself, but it could be an accomplishment if your experience as teacher of the year brought a new dimension to the learning of your students. Before beginning a portfolio, it's wise to reflect on your own involvement with families and communities to identify those things that you'd like to continue doing, those things that have little impact on student learning and can be discarded, and those things you'd like to add to your practice.

Family Partnerships

The standards for all certification areas state that accomplished teachers engage families in ongoing, interactive, two-way communication with a focus on student learning. There are four key words/phrases in this short, but very powerful sentence. Let's consider each of them separately.

Effective communication is . . .

Ongoing: Accomplished teachers realize that effective partnerships require continuous and open communication. They seek to involve families in all phases of the students' education through meaningful dialogue that is not limited to open houses and report cards. They make efforts to follow up on any issues they have previously discussed with families.

Interactive: Accomplished teachers recognize that effective communication goes well beyond notes and newsletters. Efforts are made to engage families in conversation—in person, by telephone, or by e-mail.

Two-way: Accomplished teachers invite family input and feedback and are available to families in a variety of ways. Recognizing that partners learn from each other, accomplished teachers listen carefully as families share insights about their culture, previous experiences, and family dynamics.

Focused on student learning: Central to all conversations is student learning. Accomplished teachers and families work together to maximize learning opportunities for each student.

Use the following chart to help you reflect on your own practice. Consider each of your communication strategies to determine if it is interactive, ongoing, two-way, and focused on student learning. Are there strategies you'd like to add to your practice that would enhance your communication with families?

Chart 2.11 Communication With Families

What I Do	Ongoing?	Interactive?	Two-Way?	Focus on Student Learning

Based on the previous chart, what communication strategy(ies) would you like to add to your practice? Why?

_____

_____

_____

_____

Communication Log

Many accomplished teachers keep complete records of all communication with families, logging all incoming as well as outgoing communications. If you have not already begun to do so, you might want to begin keeping such a log. You will find a sample log in the portfolio directions for the Documented Accomplishments entry. Based on the previous chart, what kinds of things would you find useful to record in your communication log?

Notes to Yourself:

_____

_____

_____

_____

Community Partnerships

Core Proposition 5 describes many of the ways that the community in which your school is located can serve as a rich resource for learning. Utilizing the community resources allows students the opportunity to see the application of many of the concepts included in the curriculum, thus making learning more meaningful for them. Whether members of the community bring their knowledge into the classroom, or classroom walls are extended to include local offices, museums, or shops, students begin to appreciate the relevance of the curriculum, gain an understanding of the local culture, and see how various parts of a community interact.

Perhaps a few examples of community partnerships would be helpful:

- A chemistry teacher invited graduate students from a nearby university to conduct experiments in the classroom and then arranged for the class to travel to the chemistry labs on campus.
- A middle school teacher arranged for his class to present a proposal for cleaning up the local lakes at a town meeting.
- A kindergarten teacher invited parents into the classroom to talk about their traditions.
- A music teacher arranged for her students to perform at a local nursing home.

How have you and your students interacted with the community? Are there additional resources in the community that you could tap?

Chart 2.12 Community Partnerships Accomplishments

Resources I've Used	Resources I'd Like to Use

Notes to Yourself:

_____

_____

_____

_____

Involvement in Learning Communities

Accomplished teachers are highly involved in a variety of learning communities, most of which stretch well beyond their classrooms. Activities might involve the classroom, grade-level, school, city, county, state, national, and/or international communities. While interacting within each of these communities, accomplished teachers may serve as leaders/collaborators (serving on committees, as officers of professional organizations, etc.) and/or as learners.

Leader/Collaborator: Accomplished teachers who serve as leaders/collaborators might publish articles about their work, develop curriculum, mentor new teachers, conduct staff development for their school district, write grants that extend their school resources, sponsor school clubs, serve as grade-level or department chairs, present at state and national conferences, or participate in any number of similar activities. Use the following chart to list ways in which you have significantly served as a leader/collaborator during the past 5 years. Beside each, note how that activity significantly impacted student learning. Are there other leader/collaborator roles you'd like to assume?

Chart 2.13 Leader/Collaborator

Things I've Done	Impact on Students	Things I'd Like to Do

Notes to Yourself:

_____

_____

_____

_____

Lifelong learner: Recognizing the need to strengthen knowledge, skills, and/or teaching practices through relevant professional development experiences, accomplished teachers are also lifelong learners. They actively pursue opportunities to learn more about their craft and/or their subject areas. Among other things, they frequently choose to attend staff development activities, read professional journals, participate in book studies, take college classes, and attend state and national conferences. Use the following chart to list things you have done in the past 5 years that demonstrate your commitment to lifelong learning. Beside each, note how that activity significantly impacted student learning. Are there other lifelong learner activities you would like to pursue?

Chart 2.14 Lifelong Learner

Things I've Done	Impact on Students	Things I'd Like to Do

Notes to Yourself:

_____

_____

_____

_____

DO YOU HAVE THE TIME?

The National Board Certification process will be a time-consuming commitment, taking anywhere from 200 to 300 hours outside the classroom to complete. Therefore time is an important issue to consider. Just as learning takes time for our students, it will take time for you as you learn about yourself through this process.

You may be asking yourself "How can I find more time in an already busy teaching schedule? How am I going to balance my personal and professional life? How will going through the process affect my family? Is there enough time in the day to fit this into my life?"

Consider this quote by Charles Burton: "You will never find time for anything. If you want time, you must take it."

As you begin to think about time and the National Board Certification process, here are some tips and suggestions for planning ahead to organize your time:

1. Hold a family meeting. Let your loved ones know what you plan to do and ask for their support. Make note of activities that each family member could do to help you take time.

2. Talk to your principal. Find out how he or she might help you through the process (provide some release time, provide some resources, reduce your leadership responsibilities, arrange for you to have an intern, etc.). Make a list of suggestions that are agreed upon at the meeting.

3. Look at your calendar. List all events, situations, or commitments that will require your time and cannot be changed (vacations, family schedules, committees, volunteer work, etc.).

4. Assess how you are currently spending your time. Look at one week. Write down everything you do. Identify areas where you might spend too much or too little time. Are there places where you can take time?

5. Make a standing date with yourself. Think about how much time you are willing to set aside each day or week. Begin to "pencil in" that time on your calendar. Consider before or after school, planning times, weekends, evenings, vacation time, or holidays. Take the time to keep your date!

Notes to Yourself:

_____

_____

_____

_____

FREQUENTLY ASKED QUESTIONS

How will I know when to use each kind of writing?

When completing a portfolio entry you will be answering a set of questions prepared by the National Board. The key to the kind of writing required to answer the question lies in the question itself. If the directions ask you to explain to tell or describe, you will use descriptive writing. If you are asked to justify a decision or to draw a conclusion about the students, you will use analysis. When discussing what you'd change about your instruction in the future (and why you'd make those changes), you'll use reflection.

Do the types of writing overlap in an entry?

Yes. In order to justify an instructional choice, you will need to describe the students, talk a bit about the choice (description), and tell how the students reacted to that choice (analysis). Because each portfolio entry requires that you discuss several teaching choices, this process will be repeated often throughout the entire entry.

Do all entries start with description, move through analysis, and then end with reflection?

Yes and no. Each entry will begin with information about your teaching situation (description) and end with a discussion of what you'd do in the future (reflection). The middle portion of each entry is not so clear-cut. Throughout this part of the entry you will describe your teaching choices and justify them within the context presented in the first section. So, even though the middle sections usually contain the word *analysis,* both description and analysis are required. To make things even more interesting, the "Reflection" section of each entry requires description (What would you do differently?) and analysis (Why?). All of this will become much clearer as we progress through the book.

How will I know if I have enough analysis in my entry?

This is a very good question—and a fairly difficult one to answer. As previously noted, oftentimes the difference between achieving National Board Certification and not achieving it is the degree to which the candidate analyzes his or her practice. After writing an entry (or a portion of an entry), it's a good idea to look for "because" statements or places where you have told why you've made your choices. If you find that most of your writing tells what you did, what the students did, or how the students responded to what happened, then your writing is mostly descriptive. On the other hand, if you find that you have looked below the surface and discussed why you created the activities, why the students reacted as they did, why the materials seemed to be the most appropriate, and so on then you will have evidence of analytic writing.

Are there sample entries I can use to help me understand all of this?

There are sample entries throughout this book as well as in the "Getting Started" section of the portfolio directions provided by the NBPTS. One of the exercises that many candidates have found helpful is to choose three different color highlighters, one color for each kind of writing. Then "color" sample entries while reading them (e.g., highlight all descriptive writing yellow, all analysis green, and all reflection pink). You might want to do this with the Core Proposition scenarios found in the first chapter of this book.

Can I start on these entries the year before I officially become a candidate?

Yes and no. All work for the classroom practice entries and the family and community portion of the Documented Accomplishments must be completed with the class(es) you are teaching during the year of application. However, the learner and leader portions of the Documented Accomplishments may include activities from the most current 5 years. Consequently, you could begin writing portions of your Documented Accomplishments prior to making application, but the other portfolio entries would have to wait.

If I teach several different classes of students each day, can I highlight more than one class in my portfolio?

Yes. In fact, it is required that each of your entries highlight different students and different units of instruction. Teaching multiple classes each day makes this requirement a bit easier to meet.

Can I complete one of the elementary generalist portfolios if I'm teaching in a departmentalized school?

Yes. Some teachers accomplish this by teaching interdisciplinary units of study. Others coteach or team teach classes with their colleagues.

Can I choose to take the content exam after I finish the portfolio?

When you become an official candidate, you will be provided a window of time in which all parts of the assessment must be completed. This includes a specific date when your portfolio must be received by the NBPTS and a period of time during which you must complete the written examination. As long as you stay within those windows, the order in which you complete each component is up to you. Some candidates choose to complete the portfolio prior to the content assessment; others choose to take the examination early in the process. Your choice will most likely be determined by how much review of content you think will be necessary, coupled with the required testing dates.

Will I be required to submit evidence in all three categories in the Documented Accomplishments?

Yes. Your work with families and community must consist of accomplishments completed during the year of application. Accomplishments in the learner and leader categories may be from the most current 5 years. Although the three categories overlap, you need not submit activities in each of the overlapping areas.

Suppose I started an activity 7 years ago and am still doing it now. Can I include that in the Documented Accomplishments?

Yes, as long as it is an activity that has significantly impacted your students and/or your teaching within the most current 5 years.

If I begin the process and find that I can't commit the appropriate amount of time to it after all, can I withdraw from it?

Yes. It's important to read all state as well as NBPTS guidelines before doing so, however, in order to avoid losing your entire application fee.

DESTINATION: NATIONAL BOARD CERTIFICATION?

You have compared your practice to the Five Core Propositions and the Standards for your certificate area, explored the three types of writing required in the portfolio, analyzed the portfolio entry requirements, read the specifications for content assessment items, and analyzed your use of time. Now it's time to put all of the pieces together to decide if National Board Certification is a good destination for you. Use the notes and charts you've completed thus far to help you answer each of the following questions. If, when you're done with this exercise, you have a large majority of "I need more time!" responses, it may be a good idea to revisit the Core Propositions and Standards for your certificate area and plan ways to infuse them into your practice. On the other hand, if you have a large majority of "Yes!" responses, you're ready to begin making plans for what will most likely be one of the most incredible journeys of your career.

Chart 2.15 Are You Ready?

	Yes!	I Need More Time!
Is your practice in line with the Five Core Propositions?		
Is your practice in line with the standards?		
Can you recognize and use all three kinds of writing?		
Will your teaching situation allow you to do all requirements of the portfolio entries?		
Are you confident about your knowledge of content?		
Do you have a repertoire of accomplishments for:		
Family and Community?		
Teacher as Learner?		
Teacher as Leader/Collaborator?		
Can you *take* the time to do your best on the entire process?		

RESPONSES TO WRITING REQUIREMENTS ACTIVITIES

Like teaching, writing the portfolio is a complex endeavor. Oftentimes the different forms of writing blend or overlap within an entry. If you find that your responses differ from those listed in the following discussion, consider the possibility that the passage reflects such a blending.

Is it Descriptive?

1. No. Although the teacher is describing the room arrangement, he is also telling why (analysis)

2. Yes. Describes factual results of a test

3. No. Teacher is making a conjecture (analysis)

4. Yes. Description of an activity

5. No. Tells why child was retained . . . and the reason is possibly a conjecture. (analysis)

Is it Analytic?

1. Yes. Tells why teacher collaborated; justifying the behavior

2. Yes. Inference—not factual

3. No. Describes an action (description)

4. No. Looks to the future (reflective)

5. Yes. Making inferences from student work

Is it Reflective?

1. No. Justification of a goal statement (analysis)

2. Yes. Considers change to lesson

3. No. Description

4. No. Justification/explanation of technique (analysis)

5. Probably no. Making inferences (analysis)

Part II

Packing Your Bags

Congratulations on choosing National Board Certification as your next professional journey! You have analyzed your practice, your skills, and your time against the National Board Standards and requirements and decided that you're ready to begin. Now it's time to make final preparations for the journey.

Let's consider the steps involved in planning any trip. Once you've decided where you want to go, you must plan your itinerary, buy your tickets, complete all necessary forms (e.g., passport application), make reservations, decide what and who to take with you, and make sure that all of the equipment you need is in working order (and that you know how to use it!). Typically, planning takes an incredible amount of time, but the better you plan before the trip, the more enjoyable that journey will be.

This section of the book will guide you through the difficult but incredibly important tasks of

1. applying to become a candidate (your ticket),

2. completing several of the many forms required throughout the process,

3. planning units of study and choosing accomplishments to document that will most effectively highlight your practice (mapping your course),

4. making a plan for completing all of it on time (the itinerary),

5. creating a support system that can make the task a bit less daunting (who will go with you?),

6. learning how to make a videotape (checking the equipment).

3

Managing Paperwork

S arah chose to wait until the last minute to teach the science unit she planned to include in her portfolio. She was considered the science expert in her school district and was confident that her unit on bubbles would be the perfect vehicle for highlighting her teaching skills. Two weeks before the portfolio was due, she finally read the directions for the science entry, only to realize that student work samples needed to be collected over a period of no fewer than 4 weeks. Needless to say, Sarah was unable to demonstrate her skills appropriately in that entry.

The activities in this chapter are designed to help you avoid situations like Sarah's while you're a candidate. You will begin with the forms that must be completed before you can be officially considered a candidate, and then move through each of the portfolio entries. At each stop along the way you will analyze the requirements, make preliminary decisions about units of instruction that would be most appropriate to use, and begin to select students that might help you demonstrate the depth and breadth of your practice. Learning the rules of the road *before* you begin the journey will go a long way toward helping you avoid unnecessary (and potentially costly) detours as you navigate the National Board Certification process.

COMPLETING FORMS

Not surprisingly, there are quite a few forms that must be completed before you are considered an official candidate, forms that are required during candidacy, and still more forms required as part of each portfolio entry. Several of these forms require your immediate attention.

Application Form

Obviously, the first form you must complete is the application form. Although the form and directions for completing it are easily found on the National Board for Professional Teaching Standards (NBPTS) Web site, please be very careful to check with your state before sending it to the NBPTS. Several states have adopted legislation that provides financial support to candidates, and with that support come a few restrictions about when a candidate can apply and through whom the application must be processed. Be sure to check to see if your state has such a program and follow their rules and time lines. In at least one state, candidates who fail to follow state guidelines must pay the entire application fee (instead of only 10% of it).

Verification Forms

After the application has been completed and processed by NBPTS, you will be sent additional forms on which you will document at least 3 years of successful teaching and receipt of an undergraduate degree. Each of these forms requires official signatures and/or official transcripts. Read them carefully and be sure to provide colleges, universities, and school systems adequate time to process the forms before your deadline. It is not until all of these forms have been received that you will be an official candidate for National Board Certification. (There is no requirement, however, that you wait until all forms are processed to begin working on your portfolio!)

Student Release Forms

Perhaps one of the most important forms required during the certification process is the release form signed by each student's parent/guardian. Once the portfolio leaves your hands it becomes the property of the NBPTS, and all use of the entries is at their discretion. The obvious purpose of the form, therefore, is to protect the privacy of the students in your classes. You must collect a form for *every* student who will be discussed in your portfolio and/or appears on one of your videotapes. Stated another way, if you do not have a signed release from a student's family, that student cannot exist in your work. These forms are available in both English and Spanish and must be kept on file after you have sent the portfolio to the NBPTS.

In order to maximize your choices, it's a very good idea to seek releases from every one of the students assigned to you before you begin the certification process. Some teachers have gotten them signed during home visits, some during open houses, some during parent conferences, and some by sending them home with the students. Whichever method you choose, please do it early.

ANALYZING ENTRIES: CLASSROOM-BASED ENTRIES

The NBPTS portfolio has been designed over time to capture the essence of as much of your teaching as possible in as few entries as possible. At the present time there are four entries, three of which showcase your classroom teaching and one that highlights your work with families and community. Let's begin with the entries that deal with classroom practice.

Sometimes an entry will require you to teach and analyze lessons that are part of a longer unit of study, and at other times you will be asked to reflect on a single lesson. One entry might require you to teach a small group of students, whereas another might require whole-class discussions. At least one of your entries will require analysis of student work samples, and others will require analysis of videotapes. When taken together, the entries assess your practice against all of the standards in your certification area, but each entry emphasizes different aspects of them. It is a very good idea, therefore, to carefully analyze the directions for each entry. Doing so will help you make several very important planning decisions . . . and prevent any surprises when you're actually writing your entry. Among other things, the directions will help you answer the following questions:

- What content must I teach?
- Over what period of time must the lessons extend?
- How many students must I teach?
- How many work samples must I collect?
- Do I need to submit a videotape?
- What standards will be assessed in this entry?
- What kinds of issues will I need to discuss?
- How will the entry be scored?

A path that many candidates have found helpful when analyzing each of the classroom practice entries is outlined in the next section. One candidate's interpretation of the directions for Entry 1 of the 2002–2003 ECYA/ENS portfolio follows a brief description of each step of the analysis.

1. Read the title

What are the key words? What clues does the title give you about content or emphasis of this entry? Write the title in your own words.

Entry title is "Assessment Informs Instruction." Key words: all three words are critical. It appears that I will need to show how I use results of assessments to make decisions about how and what to teach my students. My own title: Designing Lessons From Data.

2. Italics

This abstract of the entire entry is found on the same page as the title. It is a summary of the scoring rubric for this entry. What clues does it offer you about what will be assessed in the entry?

It appears that I will need to show how I use instruction as assessment (and vice versa?); how I use assessment to make instructional decisions; how I assess the total child.

3. Standards

Which standards are assessed in this entry? Reread the identified standards. Are there parts of each of these standards that seem more appropriate to this entry than others? Are there any standards that are assessed in this entry only?

A word of caution: When you send your portfolio to NBPTS to be scored, the entries will be separated and distributed to assessors throughout the country. As a result, each assessor will read only one of your entries. It is critical, therefore, that you address all standards identified for each entry within *that* entry.

Standards assessed: 1. Most of this standard talks about need to know entire student and to constantly seek to update that knowledge. Seems like the entire standard will be important. 2. Parts that discuss environment and need to adapt instruction to students seems important; not sure about collaborator; probably NOT advocacy. 4. Diversity; respect for ALL students; students respect each other; quality learning environment for all; probably NOT advocacy parts. 5. Decisions based on knowledge of students and content; decisions based in learning and curriculum theories. 6. Meaningful learning; critical thinking; anticipate and address potential difficulties, misconceptions, and confusions (based on assessment?). 9. ALL. 11. Aware of current instructional materials so can meet individual student needs; probably NOT colleagues, families, and community as resources. 13. ALL.

Standard 9 is only assessed in this entry.

4. Scoring rubric

This part describes how your response will be scored. What new information is presented here?

Holistic knowledge of special ed.; formulate question for one student; create/choose assessment tool; instruction based on assessed student strengths

5. What do I need to do?

What are the specific requirements about content, number of students, number of artifacts, and so on? List them here.

One student; identify need, formulate question, assessment related to question, design instruction based on assessment, assess effectiveness

Question document, assessment tool(s), written commentary (13 pages max)

6. Questions (composing the commentary)

Read and reflect on the questions you'll need to answer in this entry. What kinds of teaching experiences would help you answer these questions?

Need to collaborate with family in first assessment; need to justify choice of assessment tool (research? collaboration?); how to refine goals based on assessment results? Design instruction and tell how it addressed assessment results and how student responded to it.

7. Making good choices

Now that you have a general idea about this entry, read this section to fine-tune your ideas. List your emerging choices here.

- Which students/class might be good to highlight? What challenge(s) do they present to your practice?
  Robby—severe language deficit
  Missy—writing (maybe use technologies?)
- What might be a good lesson/unit topic? How will that topic help you fulfill the requirements (i.e., demonstrate how you meet the standards)?
  Language/literacy—good way to highlight knowledge of content, resources; lots of assessment models out there; hot topic with parents
- When might be a good time to teach the lesson(s)?
  Start gathering info at very beginning of year; continue through first grading period
- What will you be looking for when analyzing either the student work or your videotape?
  Match between student characteristics and instruction; my ability to adapt instruction based on assessment results
- What other possibilities might you explore?
  While collecting initial information, practice using instruction as assessment.

Now it's time to analyze each of the classroom-based entries in your portfolio. You will find a copy of the "What Am I Supposed to Do?" form in Resource 2 of this book. Complete one form for each of your entries.

Making Choices

While analyzing each of the classroom practice portfolio entries, you no doubt noticed that the choices you make regarding the topics you teach and the students you highlight will have a tremendous impact on your ability to provide evidence of the standards in your practice. You probably also noticed that there are some students and some topics that seem to be appropriate choices for more than one entry. Because the NBPTS typically requires that you highlight different students and use different units of study in each of your entries, the last important step in analyzing the entries is to view them as a complete package.

The NBPTS provides two excellent charts to help you make appropriate choices. You'll find the Entry Tracking Form and the Summary of Portfolio Entries in the Appendix of the introduction section of the portfolio directions. The first form will help you avoid overlapping content and/or students across your classroom practice entries. The second one is a summary of minimum requirements for all of the entries (including Documented Accomplishments). You may find these forms quite useful as you progress through the certification process.

Another choice you will make is how to complete the portfolio. Some candidates choose to complete one entry at a time, whereas others prefer to work on all of them simultaneously. If you are in the first category, the individual entry analyses completed in the last activity should be quite helpful to you. If not, you may prefer to transfer the information you recorded onto the following chart. When used in conjunction with the two NBPTS charts, you will have a complete picture of the classroom practice portion of the portfolio.

Chart 3.1 Classroom Practice Entry Analysis

Entry Title	Italics	Key Standards	Scoring Rubric	Requirements	Question Analysis	Emerging Choices

Notes to Yourself:

_____

_____

_____

_____

ANALYZING ENTRIES: DOCUMENTED ACCOMPLISHMENTS

The final portfolio entry requires that you document your efforts to develop and sustain meaningful partnerships with students' families, to develop and sustain meaningful partnerships with the community, to contribute as a leader and a collaborator with other professionals within a variety of learning communities, and to grow as a learner. Activities related to your work with communities can be drawn from the most recent 5 years of your teaching, whereas the activities related to developing partnerships with families are limited to those completed in the year of your candidacy. As an accomplished teacher you have no doubt enjoyed a number of leadership roles, been heavily involved with families and community, and participated in many activities that demonstrate your commitment to your students and the profession. Quite possibly complete documentation of all of these accomplishments could fill a book. The Documented Accomplishments entry of the NBPTS portfolio, however, requires you to tell your story completely, clearly, convincingly . . . and concisely. In fact, you will most likely be restricted to telling your story in about 12 pages. Choosing the most powerful examples of your commitment to students through your work with families and communities is certainly the most critical (and most difficult) part of completing this entry. Before doing so it's important to know what kinds of information you need to include in the entry, how the entry will be assessed, and what kinds of evidence are acceptable.

Making Choices

The first step to making appropriate choices is understanding the kinds of activities the NBPTS has identified as those that demonstrate accomplished teaching. As you completed the "Work With Families and Community" portion of Chapter 2, you explored each of the documented accomplishment categories and identified activities/strategies in your practice that illustrate your commitment to each one. Now it's time to review your work and fine-tune your understanding. Following are the three main categories included in your portfolio entry (the entry combines families and community). Reading them in conjunction with your previous work should help refresh your memory and clarify your understanding about the types of activities you might want to include in this entry. Your portfolio directions also include a very helpful Venn diagram illustrating the connections among each of the categories (somewhere near page 12 of that entry).

1. Work with families and community
   - Accomplished teachers show ongoing, interactive, two-way communication with a focus on student learning.
   - Accomplished teachers consider all students with whom they come in contact in the wider school community to be "their" students.
   - Accomplished teachers utilize community resources to enrich student learning.

2. Work as a leader and collaborator
   - Accomplished teachers serve the local, state, and/or national education communities in a variety of leadership roles (serving on committees, as officers of professional organizations, etc.). While doing so they collaborate with a variety of professionals, thus enriching the learning experiences for their students.

3. Development as a learner
   - Accomplished teachers are lifelong learners. They recognize the need to strengthen knowledge, skills, and/or teaching practices through relevant professional development experiences.

In Chapter 2 you completed several charts of accomplishments and resources that you have used in the past. After reading the portfolio directions for the Documented Accomplishments entry, it's likely that you have gained a few more insights into this important part of your portfolio. You might want to add these insights to your charts.

The second step in choosing which accomplishments to highlight in the portfolio is to study the criteria against which those accomplishments will be assessed. No matter how significant an activity seems to be, if it does not address the scoring criteria, it will be inappropriate for the portfolio. The following three steps outline a strategy for helping you make choices that most effectively showcase your practice.

Step 1. Reread Core Proposition 4, Core Proposition 5, and the standards for your certificate area that pertain to the documented accomplishments entry (listed in your portfolio directions). Write key phrases from these documents in the following chart.

Step 2. Familiarize yourself with the scoring rubric that will be used when assessing the Documented Accomplishments entry. You'll find the rubric in two parts of the portfolio directions: the italicized summary of the entry and "How Will My Response Be Scored?" Write key phrases from these sections in the following chart.

It is also important to read the "Note-Taking Guide" for the Documented Accomplishments entry found in your scoring guide. This document is used by the assessors to score your entry. If you are pursuing a new certification area, you most likely do not have a scoring guide available online. However, the Documented Accomplishments entry is identical for all certifications. Feel free to download any of the other scoring guides from the NBPTS Web site and use their "Note-Taking Guide" for this entry. Write key phrases from this document in the following chart.

Step 3. Compare key words/phrases from each of your lists from the previous steps. Complete the following chart to see how each of these documents work together to create a path for completing the entry.

Chart 3.2   Key Phrases

	Key Phrases/Words
Core Propositions and Standards	
Entry italics	
Scoring rubric	
Note-Taking Guide	

Notes to Yourself:

_____

_____

_____

_____

The third step to making appropriate choices is also a word of caution. All teachers are involved in a myriad of activities that stretch beyond the classroom. They attend professional development seminars, serve on school and county committees, sponsor student clubs, host open houses, communicate with parents, and attend professional conferences. Some of these activities are required by their employer, while others are purely voluntary; some have direct application to the classroom, while others have little or no effect on student learning; some are completed on school time and at school expense, while others require expenditure of personal time and/or money. Some of these experiences are considered accomplishments, while others are merely activities. What's the difference?

For purposes of the portfolio, a professional *activity* becomes an *accomplishment* only if it results in a significant (and identifiable) impact on student learning and it was not a requirement of your job. Perhaps two descriptions of the same activity will help clarify the difference.

Ms. Peterson: Two years ago I served on the districtwide mathematics textbook adoption committee. I wasn't paid to do this, and the committee met after school every Wednesday for 3 months. While serving on the committee, I used many of the activities found in the new textbooks in the geometry unit I was teaching. By doing so I was able to make an accurate assessment of the quality of each book and bring the latest methods and materials to my students. Even though the book I preferred was not chosen by the district, I've continued to use many of the activities from all of the books since that time. As a result I have a better understanding of many of the math concepts, and the students' test scores in math have shown a steady increase.

Is this an accomplishment? Did Ms. Peterson go above and beyond the requirements of her job? Did the activity have an impact on her teaching? Did it have an impact on student learning?

Ms. Hodge: Two years ago I served on a districtwide mathematics textbook adoption committee. I attended all 12 of the meetings, analyzed books from six different publishers, filled out all necessary forms, and participated in the final vote. Serving on this committee was an enormous responsibility and a huge commitment of my personal time. Sadly, the district chose not to adopt the book I preferred.

Is this an accomplishment? Did Ms. Hodge go above and beyond the requirements of her job? Did the activity have an impact on her teaching? Did it have an impact on student learning?

The difference between an activity and an accomplishment rests primarily on identifiable student impact. The same activity (service on a districtwide committee) resulted in an identifiable impact on the learning of Ms. Peterson's students, but there was no identifiable impact on students in Ms. Hodge's entry. It's important to note, however, that service on committees like this one could very well have impacted students throughout the district. (Do you see how?) If Ms. Hodge had realized that and addressed specifics regarding districtwide impact, her activity could also have been considered an accomplishment.

The written component of each of your accomplishments must contain three parts:

1. Description of the accomplishment

2. Discussion of why/how the accomplishment is significant

3. Evidence of impact on student learning

Review each of your Family and Community charts once again. For each activity you've listed, determine (1) if you exceeded the requirements of your job, (2) if it had an identifiable impact on your teaching, and (3) if it had an identifiable impact on student learning.

Documentation

It will be necessary for you to provide evidence for each of the accomplishments you include in your portfolio. An obvious purpose for this documentation is to prove that the activity actually occurred; but more importantly, the documentation is meant to support your discussion of the significance of the accomplishment. The documentation is not an add-on to the accomplishment, but rather an important part of it. A critical consideration when identifying accomplishments to highlight, therefore, is your ability to produce appropriate documentation for them.

Documentation can take several forms and will vary depending on the accomplishment (and your filing system!). The portfolio directions discuss three acceptable forms of documentation:

1. Artifacts: These are products of the accomplishment. They may include such things as a page from a conference program highlighting your presentation, an abstract of a grant proposal, a membership card for a professional organization, an outline of a staff development you presented, a syllabus for a class you taught at a college or university, a program from a student-led open house, a copy of a newsletter, a title page or portion of a publication, and so on.

2. Verification form: Sometimes you'll want to highlight an accomplishment that has no paper trail or for which you've misplaced the artifacts. In cases like these you'll want to ask someone to verify that the activity took place and attest to its significance. You might ask a colleague to verify a staff development course you copresented, the city mayor to verify his involvement with your class, the principal to verify that you made home visits, and so on. When choosing this option, you will describe the accomplishment and its significance on the top portion of the form, and the verifier will attest to the accuracy of the description, describe his or her involvement, and sign the form. Each verification form included in your portfolio must be signed by a different person.

3. Communication log: This is a sampling of your efforts to engage families in ongoing, two-way, student-focused communication. It is not required, but if included, it will provide the assessor with strong evidence of your efforts to build and sustain a meaningful partnership with your students' families.

Review each of the charts you completed in Chapter 2. What documentation could you use for each of the activities you've listed?

You are now familiar with the purpose of the Documented Accomplishment entry, the categories that are included, the criteria against which your entry will be assessed, the kinds of documentation that can be used, and the difference between an activity and an accomplishment. You have analyzed your own practice and listed several sets of accomplishments you might choose to highlight in the portfolio. It's time to begin the task of selecting accomplishments that best demonstrate your commitment to student learning.

You have created charts for each of the major categories (family and community, leader/collaborator, and learner).

1. Review the charts carefully and identify *one* activity from each chart that you think might be appropriate to include in your portfolio.

2. Transfer the information about that activity onto the "Documented Accomplishment Categories" chart included in your portfolio directions (about page 11 of the entry).

3. When you feel ready to try your hand at writing one (or all) of the documented accomplishments, turn to "Writing an Accomplishment" in Chapter 5 of this book.

FREQUENTLY ASKED QUESTIONS

Must I have the application and all of the verification forms completed before I can begin working on my portfolio?

No. You will not be an official candidate until all of the paperwork is in (and the fee is paid), but you may begin working on the portfolio as soon as you make the commitment to apply. The most common place for candidates to start is with Documented Accomplishments, because you can highlight events from the most current 5 years. As soon as the academic year starts, you may begin working on all of the entries.

Why would a parent/guardian choose not to sign a release form?

Sometimes it's difficult to obtain signatures on the release forms because of conflicting parent and teacher schedules, poor communication, or the fact that the student may not have taken the form home. Other reasons are more serious. Remember that the portfolio entries and videotapes will become the property of the NBPTS as soon as you mail them. That means that NBPTS reserves the right to show your tapes and/or parts of your written entries whenever and to whomever they choose (precandidate training, mentor training, publicity events, etc.). Although you will only use first names in your work, videotapes will automatically reveal the identity of the students in your class. Families wishing to protect the anonymity of their children (celebrities, those involved in custody issues, etc.) will not want to risk their child being seen in public.

What am I supposed to do with the students who don't have release forms?

As an accomplished teacher you will want to do everything you can to avoid drawing attention to the children or making them feel penalized in any way. To that end, some teachers have used these students as videographers or directors during videotaping, or they have positioned them in a part of the classroom that is not in view of the camera (but have reminded the student not to participate verbally). Teachers of very young students often send the child to another classroom to work on a special project.

What if the student I've chosen to highlight moves before I finish collecting all of the required work samples?

If a student moves before you've collected all necessary information, you'll need to choose another student to highlight. Doing so in the middle of the process can be quite unsettling. The best way to avoid problems is to collect work samples from at least twice as many students as required in the portfolio.

What if I find that the student work I collect doesn't give me the kind of information that best highlights my practice?

Once again, collecting samples from a variety of students will help prevent this situation. When I worked on my portfolio I created individual student folders for each subject area and filed all of their work throughout the year. At the open house, I told the parents that I wouldn't be sending very much work home, but that they could come to the classroom at their convenience to look through the files. At first I had thought this might work against me in regards to communication with families (Documented Accomplishments), but as it turned out, the amount of parent contact I enjoyed throughout the year increased in both volume and impact (because the students, their parents, and I were able to look at the work together). When it came time to complete my portfolio, I had all of the students' work at my fingertips. This may not be appropriate for you in your situation, but collecting samples from several students throughout the year will increase your options tremendously.

I teach a unit in the spring that would be perfect for one of the portfolio entries, but I'm afraid to wait until then to begin the entry. Should I teach the unit earlier than usual? Should I choose a different unit to highlight in my portfolio?

Only you can make this decision. As an accomplished teacher, however, you very likely teach within the standards every day. Consider the unit of instruction you'd like to highlight. What elements of that unit lend themselves so well to the standards? Are those elements also evident in other units? Can they be added to other units to make them more powerful?

Most of the things I've listed on the Family and Community charts are activities rather than accomplishments. Can I possibly score well on the Documented Accomplishments entry?

Yes. Your use of the word *most* implies that there are some entries on your chart that fit the definition of "accomplishment." Choose those to highlight in your portfolio. The key to success on this entry is not the number of accomplishments you discuss, but the quality of them.

When documenting accomplishments, is it better to use artifacts than verification forms?

Not necessarily. The important issue to consider is the extent to which the documentation you choose will enhance the presentation of the accomplishment. Sometimes a verification form may be much more powerful than a page from a program. Consider the accomplishment you want to highlight and choose the kind of documentation that best tells your story.

4

Planning
and Practicing

During the second phase of preparing for a journey, travelers determine the order in which they plan to visit their chosen locations, decide how long they want to stay in each place, learn how to use their camera equipment, gather all of the resources that will help them navigate unfamiliar territory, and become familiar with the laws of the area they've chosen to visit. Having gained knowledge about the portfolio entries, you are ready to enter the next phase of planning your journey toward National Board Certification.

PLANNING YOUR ITINERARY

Now that you have analyzed the requirements of each portfolio entry, it's time to begin to plan for completing them in a timely fashion. The Getting Started section of your portfolio directions contains several charts that will help you create a time line. There are a number of variables to consider when completing them.

Required Curriculum. Unless you are teaching in a very unusual school, it is likely that you are required to teach a specific set of concepts and competencies each year. It is also likely that you have a repertoire of units that you typically teach each year, adapting them as appropriate to meet the needs of your present students. Compare these units of study to the entry requirements you noted in your analyses of the entries. Are any of them more likely than others to demonstrate your mastery of the standards? If so, at what time of year are the units typically taught? If they're not taught before your portfolio due date, can they be taught earlier without jeopardizing student learning? Are the units of sufficient length to use? If not, can they be adapted?

Notes to Yourself:

_____

_____

_____

_____

Students. As an accomplished teacher you know that students vary from year to year as well as from student to student. Some years the students are enthusiastic and seem to catch on very quickly. At other times, you wonder if you have any teaching skills at all! Consider the disposition and achievement levels of your class(es). When will they be ready for the units/lessons you hope to highlight in your portfolio?

Notes to Yourself:

_____

_____

_____

_____

Team Planning. Are you in a school that requires you to teach specific units of instruction at identified times throughout the year (e.g., all fourth-grade classes study fractions in December)? Will you need to vary from that schedule? Will you be permitted to do so?

Notes to Yourself:

_____

_____

_____

_____

Resources. Will you need to share resources when teaching the lessons that you've tentatively chosen? If so, when will they be available?

Notes to Yourself:

_____

_____

_____

_____

School Calendar. Are there events during the school year that may prevent you from honoring the time requirements placed on units/lessons in the portfolio directions (holiday programs, competitions, athletics, testing, parent conferences, etc.)?

Notes to Yourself:

_____

_____

_____

_____

Your Schedule. Are there events during the school year that will pull you away from the students (conferences, meetings, in-services, etc.)?

Notes to Yourself:

_____

_____

_____

_____

You are now ready to complete the Entry Tracking Form and the Suggested Calendar included in the Getting Started portion of your portfolio.

MAKING A VIDEOTAPE

The National Board for Professional Teaching Standards (NBPTS) is looking for evidence of your ability to "walk your talk." Throughout your portfolio you are asked to describe, analyze, and reflect upon your practice and then provide samples as evidence supporting your comments. In some cases this evidence will be a videotape of your teaching. Before beginning these entries, it's important to realize that your videotapes are not the main event. Instead, they serve as illustrations of the points you make throughout your portfolio entry. They also provide you an opportunity to demonstrate your analytic and reflective abilities as you discuss episodes seen on the video.

Your task is not to record yourself on tape and then try to make the video fit the questions. Instead, you'll want to plan the entire entry (even write a good bit of it), videotape your teaching, and then choose the part of the video that best demonstrates the points you want to make about how you meet the standards for your certification area. Many candidates are intimidated by the videotaping experience, often saying that they'd prefer to have someone observe them in person. The good news, however, is that you will be able to choose which 15 or 20 minutes of the tape you want to submit, and you can tape as often as you'd like in order to get a segment that best illustrates the points you wish to make in your writing.

So what is the National Board looking for on your videotape? This is a very good question—but perhaps there is another one that's even better: What might they see that they are *not* looking for? And how might that affect your scores?

When you see your classroom on tape, you might be surprised by what you see. Things that you never even realized were there will jump out at you. There may be something on a shelf or on the wall that seems odd. There may be student(s) sleeping in the back. There may be some student-to-student discourse that you didn't recall happening during the lesson. Your facial expressions may betray your words, or you may find that your room looks much more inviting than you realized and that you were able to make meaningful contact with every child.

Although the next few pages emphasize such things as camera placement and microphones, the tapes you make should help you learn a great deal about your teaching. As you view each practice tape, look carefully at your classroom, your students, and yourself. Do you see evidence of the standards?

Technology Tips. The Getting Started portion of your portfolio directions contains two sections that will be quite useful to you as you prepare to videotape your teaching. The first section, Tips for Videotaping, discusses equipment and procedures that have worked well in the past. The second section, Video Practice, leads you through some practice tapes. The highlights of these sections are included in the following discussions.

■ Equipment. When preparing to make a videotape, the first thing you'll want to do is gather the proper equipment. You will need a video camera and a microphone. Some candidates use their own cameras or they borrow one from a friend. If you use a camcorder with a small tape you will also need access to equipment that transfers the images onto a standard VCR tape (check to see if your school district or local university offers this service to National Board candidates).

Many schools have video cameras available for teachers to use. If you use one that belongs to your school, you will want to find out how often it can be checked out and what the appropriate check-out procedures are. Many candidates have run into trouble when a camera wasn't available at the time they planned to videotape. You will also want to make sure you have any and all extension cords, batteries, and "plug ins" essential for filming.

It is not necessary to use a "professional" video camera, but you will want to make sure that the microphone adequately picks up your voice and the voices of your students. Sometimes the microphone on a video camera is sufficient (especially on the smaller camcorders). But other cameras may require special microphones that allow for better voice quality. These microphones are inexpensive and can be bought or rented at any electronics store. (You may want to check with the media person at your school.) If you are in a school district where a number of teachers have already attained National Board Certification, you may find that the district has purchased an external Pressure Zone Microphone™ that you can use.

■ Filming. There are at least two options for videotaping. You may choose to operate the video camera yourself with the use of a tripod. If you choose this option, you may need to make a few adjustments, *neither of which will have a negative effect on the scoring of your entry*. You may need to

1. rearrange your furniture in order to capture the majority of student faces as well as your own,

2. reposition the camera in the middle of your lesson in order to highlight your work with a small group of students.

If you feel uncomfortable taping yourself, you'll want to ask someone else to operate the camera for you (parent, colleague, professor, student, media specialist, etc.). If you choose this option, make sure the videographer knows *what* to film and *how* to film. Typically the portfolio entry requires you to capture as many student faces as possible. As inexperienced videographers attempt to follow conversations, they tend to move the camera so quickly that the viewer feels seasick when watching the finished product. Reviewing your lesson plan and your film goals with the videographer prior to your lesson will greatly assist him or her in providing you with a usable tape.

■ You and Your Students. We've all seen students act for a camera. And most of us have seen tapes of ourselves that were not accurate portrayals of our teaching because the filming made us so nervous. Neither of these situations will be useful on a National Board videotape. The purpose of the tape is to provide the assessor with evidence that you teach the way you say you teach in your written entries. It is in your best interest, therefore, for the tape to reflect a normal day in the life of your classroom. If you begin taping your class(es) early and often, you and the students will very likely become desensitized to the camera, and the likelihood of capturing accomplished teaching on tape will increase exponentially.

It's also important to note here that your videotape does not need to reflect perfect teaching. For example, when Peter mentors candidates, he recalls that when he completed his portfolio, he made six videotapes of one class before he was happy with the content. Both he and his students were very proud of the sixth tape. No one made any errors, and they all looked like they were enjoying the lesson. When it came time to discuss his videotape in the written commentary, Peter discovered that he had very little to discuss. His tape was too perfect! He laughs now when he tells candidates that the tape he actually submitted was the very first one he filmed with that class. By analyzing a lesson that was less than perfect, he was able to reflect on why things went poorly and what he planned to do in the future to avoid making the same mistakes.

The best way to learn about videotaping is to videotape. After testing a variety of cameras, microphones, classroom setups, and camera operators, you'll feel much more confident about the videotaping experience and be more likely to capture the best parts of your practice on film. Resource 3 of this book includes a Videotape Options form. As you experiment with equipment, camera angles, and camera operators, use the form to help you determine which combination of camera/microphone works best for your classroom and to note classroom characteristics. Remember to keep your tapes within the required time limit and not to tape students without release forms (you might want to use one of your practice tapes in your portfolio!).

CREATING A SUPPORT SYSTEM

By now you are probably feeling a bit overwhelmed by all that is required in the National Board Certification process and the drains that already exist on your time and resources. Please relax. No matter where you live, you will not need to make the National Board journey alone. There are a number of resources and support systems available to you, many of which are right in your own classroom. These resources include, but are not limited to, people, courses, the Internet, and e-mail.

People

You have already discussed your National Board plans with the most important people in your life and have determined how you will share personal responsibilities with them. In this section we will look beyond family to colleagues, mentors, students, students' families, administrators, and friends.

Colleagues. Accomplished teachers do not teach in a vacuum. They share their expertise with and learn from their colleagues. Perhaps your strongest support system, therefore, will be the group of teachers with whom you work every day, even if they are not themselves candidates for National Board Certification. They know the population you teach and the restrictions of your curriculum. Their proximity makes it possible for you to ask them questions, seek their advice, coplan activities, and observe each other's teaching. As you engage in conversation with them you will find that you will be able to clarify your thoughts and be better able to express them in your portfolio.

What colleague(s) could help you clarify your practice?

Mentors. You will want to find a cadre of people to mentor you through the certification process. Some of them will be National Board Certified Teachers (NBCTs).

Some will not. Some may not even be teachers! Your choice of mentors will be determined by the job you'd like the mentor to do for you. Some of the jobs that previous candidates have given to their mentors include the following:

1. Interpreter—usually an NBCT; used to clarify the National Board requirements

2. Challenger—a devil's advocate who questions your choices of methods and materials

3. Planner—a respected colleague who will help you plan your lessons

4. Task master—keeps you on your time line

5. Standards police—a cadre of people, not necessarily teachers, who are each responsible for knowing one of the standards inside and out; each person reads your work, looking for evidence of the appropriate standard

6. Editor—not necessarily a teacher; reviews your work for spelling and grammar

7. Wordsmith—helps you express your ideas clearly and concisely

8. Videographer—films your lessons

9. Outside reviewer—teacher from a different discipline; advises you on the clarity of your work

10. Cheerleader

As you progress on your journey, the types of mentoring you seek will vary. At this point, are there some tasks you already know you'll need assistance with? What are they? Who could you call on to help you? Is there someone in your school district who can recommend appropriate mentors to you?

Students and Their Families. It will be necessary for you to discuss the National Board Certification process with your students and their families before you officially begin. As you obtain permission from the families, you may find that they will be able to provide unexpected support throughout the process. It is not uncommon for parents and/or students to serve as videographers, technology advisors, challengers, and planners or to provide supplies when needed (you'll use an incredible amount of paper, for instance). But, most importantly, if they see themselves as being collaborators in the process, they can provide the emotional support you'll need throughout the year.

How/when will you elicit support from students and their families?

Administrators. The principal, assistant principal, deans, and curriculum specialists can play invaluable roles within your support system. Before embarking on the journey, make an appointment with your administrators to discuss what you will be doing and why you have chosen to do it and to decide together how they can support your efforts. Some administrators have provided several release days (at the school's expense), additional funds to help with the cost of supplies, additional supplies, and/or the assistance of paraprofessionals at "crunch" times during the process. Some have even served as substitutes when the candidates were pressed against deadlines.

How would you like your administrators to help you?

Friends. Friends can serve an incredibly important role in providing emotional and physical support throughout the certification process, but only if you keep them informed. If they are aware of the rigors of completing the portfolio, they can surprise you with baby-sitting, a casserole, a box of chocolates, or a hug.

Courses

Several colleges and universities throughout the country offer graduate courses designed to help you assess your teaching against the standards. A few schools offer candidate support courses online. If you are interested in receiving this kind of support, check the Web sites of the colleges and universities in your state to see what they offer. In addition, the NBPTS Web site includes an incomplete list of institutes of higher education that have embraced the National Board Certification process.

Internet and E-mail

There are several electronic groups (e-groups) that have been formed by and for National Board candidates. Groups are typically defined by certification area and are designed as places where candidates can share ideas, concerns, and questions about the specifics of their portfolios. Some of these groups also have NBCTs on them (they remain after achieving certification). One popular vehicle for these groups is http://www.groups.yahoo.com. Once you have reached the site, type "NBPTS" in the search box. A large number of groups will appear on your screen.

The NBPTS Web site also provides an incredible amount of support for candidates. You've already explored much of the site, but it may be worth another visit to see all of the options available to you in the Candidate Resource Center. One of the most useful parts of the site is Frequently Asked Questions, which is continually updated.

Another way to find resources to help you through the process is to search "NBPTS discussions" in any of the more popular Internet search engines (e.g., Google and Lycos).

Take some time now to explore the Internet and record sites that you think might provide the kind of support you'll require.

ETHICS

No matter how prepared you are before embarking on the National Board Certification process, you will experience moments of discomfort, confusion, concern, and frustration while completing the portfolio entries and preparing for the assessment tests. The pressures of your normal teaching load coupled with those specific to the certification process will start to build, and you may find yourself tempted to ask NBCTs for detailed information about what they wrote in their portfolios or what questions they had to answer on the content assessment test. Before putting pen to paper, therefore, it is a good idea to review NBPTS's ethics policies for candidates and NBCTs.

There are three documents on the NBPTS Web site that you have most likely already seen, but are worthy of review:

- Candidate Agreements Regarding Ethics
- Collaboration Guidelines
- Certification Denial or Revocation Policy

Sadly, these policies have been enforced on at least one occasion, resulting in severe penalties for candidates and NBCTs alike.

How will you know when you (or your mentor) are about to step over the line? Perhaps the best way to avoid unethical behavior is to become sensitive to conditions leading to it. Following are a few scenarios for your consideration. In each case, the NBCT is at risk of having his or her certificate revoked, and the candidate is at risk of being banned from the certification process.

1. Sometimes well-meaning NBCTs will offer to lend you their portfolios. Don't take them!

2. Sometimes mentors will begin a sentence with "On my test I had to . . ." Interrupt them immediately and remind them that they signed an oath not to divulge that information.

3. Sometimes candidates (and NBCTs) post their portfolio work on electronic discussion groups, hoping to receive feedback. Delete them unread!

4. Sometimes mentors will read (and rewrite) your work without discussing it with you. Ignore them! This is *your* portfolio, not theirs.

5. Sometimes well-meaning NBCTs who have scored entries in the past will volunteer to score your entry and tell you how to make it better. Although this is not blatantly unethical, it is better for you to compare your work to the standards rather than to rely on a possibly misinformed individual.

If you look carefully at these five examples you'll see that all of them have one thing in common: They all emphasize achieving certification rather than analyzing your practice. You will recall that one of the purposes of the NBPTS is to improve the quality of teaching. To that end the certification process has been designed to be a very powerful staff development experience. As you seek mentors, therefore, always look for people who will help you analyze your practice against the standards. As long as the focus is on *your practice*, you should be able to avoid the temptations that lead to unethical behavior . . . and you'll probably do well on your assessments.

FREQUENTLY ASKED QUESTIONS

If there's another adult in my classroom during videotaping, do I need to have him or her sign a release form?

Yes. Security issues are the same for adults as they are for children.

If another teacher is mentioned on the videotape, do I need to have him or her sign a release form?

Yes. Students will most likely refer to the teacher by last name, which will immediately erase all possibility of anonymity.

I'm really nervous that the quality of the videotapes may not be professional enough. Should I hire someone to tape me?

That's your choice, but it's absolutely unnecessary. Remember that the purpose of the videotape is to provide evidence that supports what you've written. The assessor will read your entire entry and then watch your tape looking for evidence of the standards in your teaching. Lighting, sound, camera angles, and so on are only important inasmuch as they allow you to show the assessor your classroom. Although the assessor will need to see faces of students, hear what they are saying, and see and hear you, there is no need to create a professional quality tape.

What if my videotape has a break in it? Can I still use it?

Probably not. Some portfolios allow (and even require) several snippets on the tape. Typically, however, that is not the case. If the directions indicate that the tape must be "continuous and unedited," that's precisely what they mean. Even if a tape has an innocent break in it, it could end up looking like you edited out something that you didn't want the assessor to see. That being said, the NBPTS has shared stories about tapes with breaks in them that were acceptable. In each of these cases, the candidate included information in the portfolio about the technical problem that resulted in the break. Unless you are bumping up against severe deadlines, however, it is always better to be safe than sorry. If your tape has a break in it, plan to tape again. Although the lesson might not be the same as the one you originally captured on tape, your teaching will still be the same. And that's what the assessor is looking for.

Does the videotape have to be perfect? What if we get interrupted (by the intercom, a visitor, etc.), a few of the students are off task, or the students don't understand the lesson? Will I need to start all over again?

Accomplished teachers seldom (if ever) have perfect lessons, perfect students, and perfect conditions. In fact, without some difficulty, it's impossible to show how you adapt to situations and to the individual needs of your students. Strive for reality, not perfection. Otherwise you may not be able to provide evidence of how you meet the standards in your teaching.

Part III

Making the Journey

Believe it or not, you have already completed the most difficult part of your journey toward National Board Certification. Quite often National Board candidates feel a bit paralyzed as they begin the assessment process. They organize their classrooms, prepare files and file boxes, talk to other candidates or National Board Certified Teachers (NBCTs), attend in-services, and generally put off the task of getting started! You, on the other hand, are ready to take the plunge!

You have studied the National Board for Professional Teaching Standards (NBPTS) Five Core Propositions and the standards for your certificate area and identified parts of your practice that demonstrate you are an accomplished teacher. You have read the directions for each of the portfolio entries and begun to devise a plan for completing them. You have studied the content knowledge assessment prompts and compared them to the knowledge you possess. And you have compared the portfolio requirements with your personal and school calendars in order to refine your plan and develop a suitable support system. In a nutshell, you now understand the standards, the requirements, and the pressures that you'll encounter throughout the year and have taken steps to ensure that you can complete the process in a timely fashion. All that's left now is the teaching and the writing! That's not to say that this part is easy—but it is, by far, the most enjoyable. You would obviously not be an accomplished teacher if you didn't enjoy working with your students. What you might not have done before is write it all down.

The purpose of Chapter 5 is to help you paint an accurate (and accomplished) picture of your practice. The purpose is *not* to tell you how to teach or to tell you what to write in order to ensure certification. Besides being unethical, such information would also be useless . . . and against all that NBPTS represents. The National Board Certification journey is one of personal and professional development. The activities, hints, suggestions, and charts in this chapter are therefore designed to help you analyze your practice against the criteria set forth by the NBPTS. By following this route not only will you refine your practice, but your chances of achieving certification will improve!

At some point in your journey you will be taking the content knowledge assessment tests. Depending upon the amount of preparation you feel will be necessary, you will choose to take the tests while you are working on your portfolio entries, or you'll wait until your portfolio is completed. In either case, you'll want to spend a bit of time anticipating the types of questions you might be asked, becoming familiar with the test format, and honing your speed writing skills. After completing activities in Chapter 6, it is hoped that you will feel comfortable with the test format and confident that you can respond to items quickly and accurately.

5

Creating Your Portfolio

You will recall that there are two different types of entries included in your portfolio: Classroom-based entries (which provide evidence of your daily teaching practice) and Documented Accomplishments (which demonstrate your commitment to families and community). Even though both the intent of each of these categories and the writing required in them differ significantly, all of them begin with a Contextual Information Sheet. Many candidates choose to begin writing their portfolio with this form.

The Documented Accomplishment entry usually takes a great deal more time than candidates expect. Not only must you write about each accomplishment (telling how it was significant and how it impacted students), but you must provide appropriate documentation for each one. Looking though files and/or retrieving verification forms from colleagues can be remarkably time-consuming tasks. It is therefore a good idea to start this entry early.

That is not to say that you should wait until you've completed the Documented Accomplishments entry to begin working on the other entries. On the contrary, you will want to begin teaching the lessons, collecting work samples, and making videotapes as soon as possible. As previously discussed, some candidates prefer to complete one entire entry before beginning the next. Others prefer to work on all of them simultaneously. No matter what your preference, before you can write about your teaching, you must teach! And the more you plan your teaching around the standards that will be assessed, the easier it will be to write the entry. Activities in Chapter 5 are designed to help you collect evidence of your teaching, analyze that evidence against the standards and requirements of your portfolio, and tell your story with the appropriate amount of description, analysis, and reflection.

CONTEXTUAL INFORMATION SHEET

You will be required to submit a Contextual Information Sheet with every portfolio entry (even the Documented Accomplishments). This is the reader's first look at you and your teaching environment. As such it provides you with an opportunity to mentally prepare him or her for your entries. You will find the form in each of the entry directions. If you teach in several schools, you will be required to complete a separate form for each of the schools you highlight. If you are not an itinerant teacher, however, you will complete only one of these forms and attach a copy of it to each entry.

Find the requirements for the Contextual Information Sheet in your portfolio directions and read them carefully. You will probably be required to write two paragraphs containing information about your teaching context that you believe would be important for the reader to know in order to understand your entries. In the first paragraph you'll be limited to telling about the organization of your school, but you'll have a bit more freedom in the second paragraph. In this section you might include details of any district or state mandates (such as required curricula, assessments, pacing, or texts) that influence your teaching, the backgrounds of your students, the type of community in which your teaching occurs, the amount of parent involvement your school enjoys, the resources available to you (or not available to you), and any other information that you think will help the reader understand your teaching situation. You may need to consult with your attendance clerk and/or school administrator to obtain some information such as number of students in the school, percent of students on free and reduced lunch, and so on. It's important to remember that the sole purpose of the Contextual Information Sheet is to prepare the reader for the broader context in which you practice. You will be asked to describe specific classes or students that you will be highlighting at the very beginning of each entry, so you will not include that information on this form.

A word of caution: Sometimes candidates inadvertently trigger biases of their assessors in the Contextual Information Sheet by seeming to complain about their teaching situation. Instead of stating the facts ("93% of students in the school are on free or reduced lunch."), they might place a value judgment on the facts ("Teaching at my school is very challenging because 93% of students are on free or reduced lunch."). Please remember that this paper is the reader's first impression of who you are as a professional.

Use a blank sheet of paper to record all of the information that you think is necessary to help the reader understand and appreciate your teaching context. After you have written the information you think is important, complete the following steps:

1. Copy the form from your portfolio directions.

2. Place your information in the space provided on the form (single spacing is allowed).

3. Check to be sure you have not inadvertently included words or phrases that could trigger reader biases.

When it all fits, you will have completed your first portfolio task!

DOCUMENTED ACCOMPLISHMENTS

Many candidates find the Documented Accomplishments entry to be terribly difficult to write . . . first, because teachers as a whole are not comfortable talking about themselves and their accomplishments (i.e., bragging), and second, because the bottom line must always be significant impact on students. As you write a few accomplishments, you'll become more comfortable with the requirements and the format. You'll also find that some of the activities you thought were accomplishments were not as significant as you had originally believed. This entry takes a great deal of time and thought, so let's get started!

Writing an Accomplishment

The written portion of each of your documented accomplishments must contain three parts. There is a detailed discussion of each section in your portfolio directions. Following is a listing of the highlights.

1. What is the nature of the activity? In this section you will describe the activity very clearly so that people who don't know you or your teaching situation will be able to "see" what you've done. You will tell what you did, why you did it, when you did it, how you were chosen to do it, and any other details about the activity that will help the assessor appreciate the breadth and depth of the accomplishment. (You will use descriptive writing in this section.)

2. How is the activity significant? It is in this part of the entry that you will tell *how* the activity exceeded the requirements of your job and/or reached beyond the routine and *how* the accomplishment demonstrates your work with families and community, as a leader/collaborator and/or as a learner. (You will use mostly analytic writing in this section.)

3. How has the activity impacted student learning? You will use both description and analysis as you tell how this activity impacted teaching and/or student learning. It is important to be quite specific, citing examples or presenting data that clearly show the connection between the activity and student learning.

The final consideration when writing each entry is the documentation. What documentation will you use for the activity? How will you get it?

In Part II of this book (Planning the Journey) you analyzed your practice and listed several sets of accomplishments that you thought you could highlight in your portfolio. After reviewing your "Documented Accomplishments Categories" chart (included in your portfolio directions), revisiting descriptive and analytical writing and rereading the details included in your portfolio directions, you'll be ready to begin writing your accomplishments. Use "Writing an Accomplishment," identified as Resource 4 of this book, to help organize your thoughts for each accomplishment. Perhaps the following excerpt from this form will help guide your thinking.

Home Visits

What is the nature of the activity? [Detailed description]

- *Goal is to visit each student before school starts in fall*
- *Letter of introduction precedes visit; appointment made via telephone*
- *Agenda of visit: introduce myself; learn about student and family; take photograph of student holding object that means a lot to him or her; give student (and family) letter describing the class and including a class list*

How is the activity significant? [How is it beyond routine, what is the impact, how does it address category(ies) and standards?]

- *Not required by school district or principal*
- *Met with 16 of 20 students before school started; rest were on vacation and met with me in their homes during the first week of school*
- *Standards: communication, impact of family on learning; development of rapport with families; families as partners; respect for student diversity; assess student interests; teach whole student*

How has the activity impacted student learning? [Be specific.]

- *Students came to school relaxed; not strangers*
- *Family involvement—90% of families came to open house; more than half families volunteer in classroom; open lines of communication (phone, e-mail, visits) developed*
- *Students came to school knowing that they were partners in their own education (along with their families and me); students readily accepted responsibility for their learning (helped set goals, student-run parent conferences, etc.)*
- *Classroom community developed more easily than before used home visits; students came to school trusting me and knowing that I respected them as individuals*

What documentation will you use for the activity? [How will you get it?]

- *Schedule of visits signed by the principal*
- *Copy of note from Mrs. C. written after the visit*
- *Copy of note from Meg written in Christmas card*

A word of caution: It is entirely possible that as you're writing an accomplishment, you will decide that the activity isn't as significant as you had thought it was. Do not despair . . . and do not destroy your first efforts. As you write more accomplishments, you will begin to feel comfortable with the format and more adept at discussing (and discovering) significance.

There is no magic number of accomplishments required in the portfolio. The only restriction is that you must include something from each category, and you must limit your work to a specified number of pages.

For this entry "less is more." There is no need to feel pressured to include a large number of accomplishments in the entry. A few highly significant accomplishments will result in a much more powerful portfolio than a great many marginal ones.

Reflective Summary

When you have described, analyzed, and documented all of your accomplishments, it will be time to begin work on the reflective summary. Although the summary is limited to two pages in length, it is usually considered to be quite challenging. It is in this portion of the entry that you answer the question "So what?" about your accomplishments.

What Is a Reflective Summary?

The accomplishments you have documented in this entry represent a small part of who you are as a professional. Typically the accomplishments are disjointed, isolated events in your life as a teacher. It is in the reflective summary that you are given the opportunity to show how all of these activities blend to make you an accomplished teacher.

In the reflective summary you are asked to reveal patterns that have emerged throughout your career. Each of us is unique, and as professionals we usually have a career agenda or goal. Consciously or unconsciously we tend to gravitate toward activities that help us reach those goals. What career goals have you been working toward? I suspect that even if you've never asked yourself this question, when you reread the activities you've chosen to highlight in this entry, you'll discover them.

How are these patterns found?

Reread all of your documented accomplishments. In what way(s) are they alike? How are they different? How do they collectively show your commitment to student learning?

Reflect on your work with families and community. What has been your role in developing and sustaining partnerships? Are your leadership, collaborative, and/or learner qualities involved?

Reflect on yourself as a leader/collaborator in your accomplishments. Have you found yourself taking on leadership roles throughout the activities? If so, did the leadership role change depending on the situation you were in?

Consider your commitment to lifelong learning. How is that revealed in your accomplishments? Do you have to take classes to show this commitment? In what other ways was this commitment illustrated?

Consider the various communities you've served in your accomplishments. In what way(s) are they alike? Different? What does the variety of communities you've served tell about you as a professional?

Consider the "well-roundedness" of your accomplishments. Do you tend to favor one form of involvement over another? Is anything missing?

Questions That Must Be Answered in This Section

The portfolio directions indicate that you must answer three sets of questions when considering the overall significance of your accomplishments:

1. What patterns do you see emerging from the accomplishments that you chose to describe and document?

2. In your work outside the classroom, what was most effective in improving student learning? Why? What would you do differently if you had the opportunity?

3. When you look at your completed set of Description and Analysis and documentation, what does it suggest about your work as a learner, within the profession and with students' families and community in support of student learning?

Remember: The impact of your activities on student learning is the key to this entry. The final section of the Note-Taking Guide directs the assessor to consider *how you further student learning through your work with families and community, as a leader/collaborator and as a learner.*

Have you done that? If so, write your reflective summary and you'll be done with this entry.

WRITING AN ENTRY

Writing a classroom practice portfolio entry, like any writing experience, is a recursive activity. You will write, rewrite, edit, reedit, and maybe even start over once or twice. But please don't be concerned. As you refine your thoughts and words, the true picture of your teaching will emerge, both in your mind and on your paper.

There are at least two reasons the classroom-based portfolio entries are challenging to write:

1. You are expected to tell your own story, but you're provided with a predetermined set of questions you must answer when doing so.

2. You are severely restricted in the number of pages you can use to tell your story.

Quite often candidates wish they could write an essay about their teaching and send it to NBPTS to be evaluated against the standards. Upon further reflection, however, almost everyone agrees that writing to a common rubric ensures fairness, uniformity, and consistency in the certification process.

Although each classroom-based entry emphasizes a different part of your practice and asks you to answer a different set of questions, all entries are based on the same logical path. You will start with a description of the instructional context of the lesson or unit you are highlighting in the entry, move through the planning and teaching stages, and end with a reflection on the content, the students, and yourself. On the surface that sounds fairly straightforward and linear, but like all good teaching, it is neither. Let's look at how each of the pieces of a typical entry fit together to form a cohesive picture of your practice.

Instructional Context. In this portion of the entry you will discuss what you knew *before* you planned and taught your lesson/unit (and on which you based all of the subsequent instructional choices). Before you teach any lesson, you undoubtedly consider the curriculum you want (or need) to present, the students you will be teaching, and the conditions or setting in which you will teach. Although you can adapt it to fit your setting and your students, the choice of curriculum is usually not your own. It is important, however, for you to be able to tell why that part of the curriculum is important to learn at the age/stage of your students (i.e., all teachers teach required curriculum, accomplished teachers can justify doing so).

The students are a critical part of your teaching context. Who are they? How old are they? What prerequisite skills do they have regarding the content you hope to teach? Are there any learner characteristics that will impact the materials and methods you can choose to use? What is the personality of the class? How might that impact your choices?

The final consideration in the instructional context is the setting in which you will teach the identified content to those students. Some examples include the time of day you'll teach the lesson, the resources available to you, the number of students in the class, the size and configuration of your classroom, and the length of the class period.

A word of caution: Many candidates incorrectly assume that they should use the same instructional context for each of their entries. Even in a self-contained elementary classroom, this will probably not be the case. Key words in each of the portfolio directions regarding the instructional context are "that influenced your . . . (planning, choice of materials, etc.) . . . for *this* instruction." In this section you are providing the background information necessary to understand all of your choices about the unit of instruction you are highlighting in the entry. Consequently you'll want to restrict all information in this part to the curriculum, characteristics, and conditions that led you to make decisions for that unit of study only. All other information will be irrelevant (and take up much needed space!). Perhaps an example will help clarify this very important point. Following is an excerpt from the Instructional Context portion of the literacy entry from an EC Gen portfolio.

Tameka is repeating second grade this year. Her scores indicated that she entered my class reading on a first grade level. She was able to decode words fairly well, but her comprehension was incredibly poor. Her previous teacher noted that she was unable to complete any library books on her own last year and that she was frequently withdrawn during reading instruction. Tameka's math scores indicated that she excelled in computation—especially in addition and subtraction. She was also able to name and draw a variety of shapes and count by twos, tens, and fives without difficulty.

The remainder of the entry discussed the methods and materials used to help Tameka improve her reading and writing skills, with no further mention of mathematics. As you can see, the Instructional Context included irrelevant information about Tameka's math background—and neglected to include critical information needed to understand the teacher's decisions regarding writing instruction.

Planning (for Instruction). The second section of almost every entry asks you to discuss the planning process you used when designing the highlighted unit of instruction. You will be asked to describe the methods, materials, and activities you hoped to include in the lesson and justify each of your choices based on the information you presented in the instructional context. Key words in the portfolio directions are "for these students" and "at this time." After reading this section the assessor should be convinced that you know your students, the content, and any other variables that may affect student learning and that you can design appropriate instruction based on that knowledge. Stated another way, the reader should feel that your choices are logical and academically well grounded.

Analysis of (Instruction, Student Work, Videotape, Assessment). The third part of an entry requires you to thoroughly analyze your teaching. It is here that you will talk about how your activities furthered student learning (or not), how you probed students' thinking, how you addressed misunderstandings the students may have had during the activities, etc. You will tell what you did (which may actually be different from what you had planned to do), why you did it, and how well the students understood the lesson. Sometimes you will be asked to analyze a piece of student work, making inferences about that student's learning. Sometimes you will be asked to analyze your practice as shown on a videotape. Sometimes you will be required to analyze a particular teaching strategy you chose to use. In all cases, you will need to refer back to the instructional context and planning sections in order to ensure that there is a logical flow within and between all parts of your practice. Once again, the reader should feel that your analysis is logical and academically well grounded.

Reflection. The final section of every portfolio entry is a reflection. It is in this section that you will tell what you learned about the students, the curriculum, and yourself and what you plan to do with this new knowledge. You will identify parts of your instruction that worked particularly well and present evidence that supports your conclusions. You will also identify parts that you think could have been done differently, telling how you'd do them in the future, and what you'd expect the result to be. All conclusions and recommendations must, once again, be logically drawn from the information presented in the first three portions of the entry.

As you can see, your portfolio will be a tightly woven story about your classroom practice. Your task is to lead the reader through your decision-making processes so carefully that he or she is never surprised by a decision, recommendation, or conclusion you make about your students, your curriculum, or yourself. To achieve this goal, your entries must be clear, consistent, convincing . . . and logical. The following pages will guide you through each part of your Classroom-based entries.

Understanding the Questions

As noted in Chapter 2, writing a portfolio entry is like telling a story based on a rubric. Although the story you tell will be unique to your practice, the format for telling it has been standardized. To that end, your portfolio directions contain very specific sets of questions that you *must* address within each entry. Understanding those questions is therefore a critical part of writing an entry.

As you scan the classroom-based entry directions you'll notice that the questions are written in italics, while information clarifying the questions appears in standard format. Many candidates have made the grievous error of answering only the italicized questions. As a result, they failed to present the evidence required to show that their teaching was in line with the standards. As noted previously, analysis is not only the most difficult of the three kinds of writing required in your portfolio; it often determines whether or not a teacher achieves National Board Certification. The nonitalicized portion of the questions will be very helpful to you as you seek to include analysis in your portfolio. Perhaps a few examples will clarify this point.

From AYA Science 2002–2003 cycle:

What are the central features of the three segments selected for the videotape? Explain how the three segments support different aspects of the inquiry process.

Chart 5.1 AYA Science Prompt Analysis

Prompt	What I Must Do
What are the central features of the three segments selected for the videotape?	**Describe** my videotaped segments.
Explain how the three segments support different aspects of the inquiry process.	**Analyze** the three segments; tell **how** they are related to the inquiry process.

From EA Math 2002–2003 cycle:

Identify what you consider to be critical moments or choices you made during instruction that impacted the direction of the lesson. Describe the events and state why they were important. Assess how they impacted the discourse.

Chart 5.2   EA Math Prompt Analysis

Prompt	What I Must Do
Identify what you consider to be critical moments or choices you made during instruction that impacted the direction of the lesson.	**Describe** critical moments in my teaching.
Describe the events and state why they were important. Assess how they impacted the discourse.	**Justify** that these are critical moments; **make inferences** about how they affected the lesson.

From EMC PE 2002–2003 cycle:

What techniques did you use to engage specific groups or individuals and promote equitable access to learning? How do interactions in the videotape illustrate your ability to help students achieve these goals?

Chart 5.3   EMC PE Prompt Analysis

Prompt	What I Must Do
What techniques did you use to engage specific groups or individuals and promote equitable access to learning?	**Describe** teaching strategies that engaged students; **describe** strategies that provide equal access to all students.
How do interactions in the videotape illustrate your ability to help students achieve these goals?	Cite examples that **demonstrate** the effectiveness of these strategies; tell **how** I know they were effective.

Charting your portfolio requirements will make it much easier to write and edit each of your entries. Use "The Main Idea," Resource 5 in this book, to identify the main idea of each prompt and the type of writing required to respond to it. Feel free to make as many copies as needed to completely analyze all of your entries.

Dealing With Ambiguity

Now that you have read and analyzed the questions included in all of your portfolio entries, it's time to think about answering them. As you studied the questions you most likely discovered that they are somewhat ambiguous. That is to say, some candidates may interpret them differently from others. Although you may find this frustrating at first, it is this uncertainty that makes the process such an incredibly powerful professional development tool. There are at least two very effective strategies for dealing with the ambiguity of the portfolio prompts: identify and define key words and phrases within each prompt and collaborate with respected colleagues.

Defining Terms. All teachers are familiar with educational jargon, but not all teachers interpret the jargon in the same way. For example, consider the phrase "learning goals." What does it mean to you? If you were asked to tell what your learning goals were for a given unit of instruction, how would they be different from instructional goals, long-term goals, appropriate goals, overarching goals, or worthwhile goals? All of these adjectives appear throughout the NBPTS entry prompts. How will you know what to talk about? Generating definitions of key terms is an essential component of writing any entry.

Identifying key words and phrases to define, however, is not as straightforward as it would seem. Take the word *lesson,* for example. Even though it is quite possibly one of the most frequently used terms in education, it becomes fuzzy when it appears in a prompt. Is it a single teaching episode? Is it a unit of instruction? Is it the same thing as an instructional sequence? Now consider the word *methods.* Are *methods, procedures,* and *strategies* synonyms? How do goals differ from objectives? What's the difference between concepts, processes, and skills? What is feedback? Is it always a product of assessment? Are students "engaged" when they're on task? Oftentimes candidates are in the midst of writing their final draft before they begin to realize the nuances included in the prompts. Finding and defining terms early will prevent confusion and frustration later on.

Use the "What Does It Mean?" chart located in Resource 6 of this book to list key terms or phrases in each of your entry prompts. Consult the Glossary of Portfolio-Related Terms (located in the Getting Started section of your portfolio directions), the Five Core Propositions, and the standards for your certificate area to help generate definitions.

Conversations With Colleagues. You will recall that Core Proposition 4 defines accomplished teachers as those who seek the advice of others while making difficult choices that test their judgment. Given the complexity of the National Board Certification process, there is possibly no better time to engage respected colleagues and mentors in conversation.

Conversations can be formal or informal, topic specific or general, lengthy or very short. They can take place in a meeting, in a classroom, in the hallway, on the Internet, at a restaurant, or on the playground. The important thing is to talk and to talk often. Sharing strategies, debating issues, and defending your position on a variety of controversial topics will enable you to

- refine definitions of key portfolio terms and phrases,
- question your practice,
- verbalize the reasons for your instructional choices,
- clarify your thoughts about teaching and learning.

What issues would you like to discuss with your colleagues that would assist you in dealing with the ambiguity of the portfolio directions?

Finding Evidence

As you completed each of the charts in this section you no doubt noticed that every entry requires you to present clear evidence that supports and defends your instructional choices, conclusions and recommendations. Without sufficient evidence that you "walk your talk," your words, no matter how much they sound like the ones found in the standards, will not convince the reader that you are an accomplished teacher. Presenting evidence is so important that it has been suggested that "Where's my evidence?" should be the mantra of all candidates seeking National Board Certification.

You have already explored a variety of forms that evidence can take and have identified evidence of the standards in small, videotaped segments of your teaching. Now it's time to determine what specific evidence would be most suitable to use in each of your portfolio entries. We'll consider the student work samples and videotape evidence separately.

Student Work Samples. Finding evidence in student work is most easily accomplished by carefully analyzing the entry prompts against the standards and what you know about your content area. You have already identified what you must do in order to respond to each prompt in your student work entry ("The Main Idea"). Identifying appropriate evidence requires you to ask "How can I show that?" or "How can I do that?" for each of the items in the Analysis of Student Work section of the entry. Perhaps an example will help.

Chart 5.4   AYA ELA Prompt Analysis

Prompt	What I Must Do	Finding Evidence
What characteristics of the selected work samples demonstrate the student's ability to understand and interpret text?	**Analyze** student response to text	**How/Where** is "understanding" demonstrated in this student's response to the reading passage? What different ways could the text have been interpreted? What does this student's interpretation indicate about his learning?

Find all prompts related to analysis of student work on your "The Main Idea" chart. Beside each one, list several questions that will help you identify the most appropriate evidence to include in your entry.

Videotape Evidence. It is important to remember that the purpose of the videotape is to provide evidence that supports the choices, conclusions, and recommendations you've included in your written commentary. The assessor will read the entire entry and then view the video to make sure that there is a match between what you say you do and what you actually do.

The procedure for finding evidence on your videotape is much the same as finding it in student work samples. It is just a bit more complicated. First, you'll need to identify what the videotape is supposed to show. The prompts included in the analysis section of the written commentary (see "The Main Idea") and the "Making Good Choices" section near the end of each entry provide excellent guidance in identifying the teaching standards required on your tape. Once you've identified what you need to show, you'll need to decide how that could look or sound in a classroom.

The following chart illustrates the first two steps of this process using the MC Gen 2002–2003 portfolio.

Chart 5.5   Finding Evidence

Requirement	It could look like . . .	It could sound like . . .
Meaningful engagement	On-task behavior; furrowed brow; concentration	Working hum; students asking questions; students collaborating
Lesson includes both math and science	Collecting and organizing data; looking for trends	Kids using both math and science vocabulary

The final step to finding evidence is to view your tapes, looking for the behaviors you've identified.

Important note: Although each portfolio is a bit different, most tapes are limited to 15 minutes in length. Typically the tape you submit need not start at the beginning of a lesson, nor end at the conclusion of the lesson. Instead, you will be able to choose the most significant 15 minutes to submit as evidence. As you view each tape, carefully note the number on the counter for each piece of evidence you find. Your most significant 15 minutes will be that portion of the tape that contains the greatest amount of evidence.

Use the "Finding Videotape Evidence" chart identified as Resource 7 of this book to help you find evidence in your videotapes.

Including Evidence in the Entry

By now you should have analyzed each of your entries, taught the required lessons, and identified and gathered appropriate evidence. Welcome to the final stages of writing an entry! You are quite literally almost done. The charts that you've completed throughout this journey contain all of the information you'll need to answer the questions thoroughly and insightfully. All that's left now is the writing.

There are a few important points to keep in mind when writing an entry:

1. It is critical that each of your entries be written in your own voice. Even though all candidates in the same certificate area will be responding to the same questions, no two portfolio entries should sound alike. There is no "cookie-cutter" portfolio or writing formula that will ensure certification. In fact, many assessors report that entries lacking passion and voice quite often miss the mark altogether. That is not to say that you should submit a creative writing essay. You must answer the questions, and it's a very good idea to answer them in the order they appear in the directions. Just be careful not to lose yourself in the process. Perhaps an example will help make the point.

Chart 5.6 Using *Your* Voice

Lost Voice	Voice
The skills addressed in this period of instruction are creative expression through movement, music, and words. This supports the theme because the children will role-play holiday traditions through dance, music, and expressing what they have learned through writing, creating costumes, and painting murals.	The skills addressed in this period of instruction are creative expression through movement, music, and words. Because of the rich variety of holiday traditions around the world, this theme naturally allows for role-playing, dance, music, creating costumes, and painting murals. At the conclusion of our study the children will express what they have learned through writing and original works of art, thus helping these very young children develop an appreciation for writers and artists in society.

2. The reader can assess only what you've written. This sounds pretty obvious, but it's a point worth making. The readers of your portfolio entries will be teachers (not necessarily NBCTs) who are certified to teach the same age and content covered by your certificate area. For example, all assessors who read AYA Science entries are high school science teachers and all readers of MC Gen portfolios teach children between the ages of 8 and 12. Because the assessors know so much about the age and grade you teach, it would be easy for them to fill in any blanks that you may have left in your writing. It is important for you to know that they are carefully trained *not* to do this! It is imperative, therefore, that your written commentaries include all information necessary to make judgments about how well you meet the standards. The assessors will not assume that your choices are well-founded and logical. Unless you tell them otherwise, they will have to assume that your good teaching is the result of good fortune rather than good planning.

3. You will not earn points for examples of good teaching if you don't address them. Again, this seems pretty obvious, but it bears mentioning. Let's use a videotape as an example. As an accomplished teacher you will no doubt display a myriad of excellent teaching behaviors on your videotape. Some of them will be more significant than others, of course, but many of those behaviors might explain the success of the lesson you're discussing in your entry. If you do not talk about them in your written entry, the assessors will be forced to conclude that you didn't realize they were significant. Once again, your good teaching would seem to be the result of good fortune rather than informed choices.

4. You may lose points for ignoring evidence of questionable choices. Once again, let's consider a videotape. Suppose the majority of your videotape includes wonderful examples of how you ensure equity and fairness in your classroom, but there is a moment when you seem to devalue one of the more challenging students in the class (you ignore him, position yourself so that your back is to him, roll your eyes in his direction, etc.). Perhaps there is a very good explanation for this behavior that is in keeping with the standards. If so, it must be addressed. Or perhaps you

really were dismissive. As you reflect on your teaching in the entry, you'll want to address what you observed, how you feel about what you observed, and how you will improve. If you ignore the situation altogether, the assessors will have to assume that your inappropriate actions are an accurate picture of your teaching.

5. Evidence and justification are the keys to success. This has been mentioned in several places throughout the book but it cannot be overstated. Unjustified choices do not reflect your thought processes and are therefore not valued. Study the following samples to see how evidence and justification enhance an entry.

Chart 5.7 Justifying Your Choices

Incomplete	Better
When I saw that Dick was tuning out of the conversation I asked him a question to try to draw him back in.	Wanting to draw Dick back into the conversation, I asked him if he agreed with the group. He merely nodded. If I had asked him a more powerful question (e.g., What clues did you see that could lead us to this conclusion?) he would have had a better chance to rejoin the conversation, and I would have had a better chance to assess his understanding of the content.
In the future I would arrange to have a guest speaker visit the classroom.	Although they enjoyed the unit on the skeletal system, the students were frustrated that all of their resources were two-dimensional. In the future I will arrange to have an orthopedist visit the classroom to illustrate how the bones work together and to answer the students' questions about sports medicine and orthoscopic surgery.
These goals are appropriate for my students because they are required by our state curriculum.	These goals are appropriate for my students because they have mastered 3-D shapes, and each of the 2-D shapes we'll be studying can be derived from them.
Lynn's persuasive essay reveals that she has begun to combine her knowledge of science and social studies concepts.	Lynn's essay reveals that she has begun to combine her knowledge of science and social studies concepts. Although she admits that the presence of the green iguana could have devastating effects on the brown iguana, she questions the cost of removing them and the physical possibility of doing so.

It's Time to Write . . . Almost!

Following are a few reminders and suggestions to help you get started on your writing.

1. You will be assessed on your teaching, *not* on your students' achievement. Certainly there is a link between accomplished teaching and student achievement, but we all know that some of the most interesting challenges we face each year are not the students who learn easily or well. By design, you will be highlighting students who present some kind of challenge to your practice. Doing so will enable you to demonstrate the breadth of your knowledge and skill as a teacher.

2. Answer *all* of the questions. This cannot be stated often enough. The prompts included in your portfolio directions have been carefully designed to reflect the standards being assessed. Very often candidates copy all of the prompts into a word processing document, leaving spaces between each bulleted question. They then write their first draft by answering each of the questions in those spaces (using "The Main Idea" as a guide). As they refine their work in later drafts, they typically remove the questions in order to meet page restrictions. It is not uncommon, however, for candidates to leave the questions in the final draft if they have the luxury of space. Even if you choose not to use this technique, you will find "The Main Idea" chart quite helpful when answering each of the questions.

3. Ignore suggested page limits when writing your first draft. Write everything that comes into your mind. You can (and will) refine your thoughts during the editing process.

4. Suggested lengths are only suggestions. You'll note that at the end of each section, the NBPTS has provided you a suggested page limit for that section. Do not misinterpret those suggestions as mandates. The only mandate is the restriction on the total number of pages you can include in your entry. The suggestions in each section are there to help you understand the relative importance of that section within the context of the entire entry. For example, if the suggested page length is 4 and you are allowed only 12 pages for the entire entry, this is a pretty important section! On the other hand, if the suggested length is 1 page, try not to write 4 pages in that section.

Now you're ready to write your entries. Remember to use all of your charts, notes, standards, and mentors while writing.

Editing an Entry

Before submitting an entry, it's important to make sure that it reflects the standards, meets NBPTS requirements, is easy to read, and is in your own voice. You'll want to check it for content:

- Have you answered all of the questions thoroughly?
  The Main Idea
  Portfolio directions

- Does your entry show evidence of accomplished teaching?
  Introduction to the entry (the italicized portion of the directions)
  How Will My Response Be Scored?
  Note-Taking Guide
  Standards

- Is your entry tightly woven?
  Logical
  All decisions are based on evidence

- Is your entry in your own voice?
  Would a colleague know it was your entry if he or she found it in the lounge?

Although your entry will not be scored based on grammar, spelling, and sentence structure, you'll want to make sure that you communicate effectively with the assessor. To that end, it's a very good idea to check the mechanics of your entry:

- Is your entry easy to read?
  Sentence structure/grammar
  Spelling

Checking your entry against the requirements set forth by NBPTS is the last (but certainly not the least) consideration when editing. Rules regarding margins, font size, and the like are very serious. It's probably not a good idea to obsess over them, but if they aren't followed there can be serious ramifications. Consequently, it's important to check your submissions against the NBPTS guidelines:

- Does your entry meet NBPTS requirements?
  Font
  Margins
  Placement of candidate number
  Page numbering
  Total number of pages

Use the "Editing Checklist" identified as Resource 8 of this book to edit each of your entries.

PUTTING IT ALL TOGETHER

By now you have written all of the required entries and are probably quite anxious to get them out of your house. Doing so requires one final (but rather tedious) step . . . packaging the entries. At the present time, all entries are sent to NBPTS in a single box. There is some talk, however, that in the future, candidates will have the option of sending their entries separately and/or electronically. The following information reflects the state of the art in 2003. Please heed, adapt, or ignore it as appropriate.

You should have received specific packing instructions with your portfolio materials. It is critical that you follow these instructions *to the letter*. After your materials arrive at the warehouse, they will be removed from the box, and each of the portfolio entries will be sent to a different location to be scored. It is critical, therefore, that every piece of your work be labeled correctly and that all transmittal forms be completed properly and placed in the correct folders. The NBPTS directions are incredibly thorough, so it is unnecessary to repeat them here. It is appropriate, however, to warn you that packing the box takes a great deal more time than most candidates anticipate. Be sure to reserve the equivalent of at least one full afternoon for this important last step. If you have been working with a group of colleagues, family, friends, or mentors throughout the process, it might be fun to have a "box packing party," complete with music (soothing, of course!), munchies, photographs, and a visit by the Federal Express agent. Sending the materials to NBPTS is a momentous occasion: Celebrate your accomplishment!

FREQUENTLY ASKED QUESTIONS

Do I need to complete a Contextual Information Sheet for each of the classes I teach?

Probably not. The Contextual Information Sheet is used to describe the school setting in which you teach. Unless you teach in several different schools, one form can be used for all of the portfolio entries.

This is my first year at this school. Should I use a different Contextual Information Sheet for the Documented Accomplishments entry because most of the activities were done elsewhere?

That's a very good question. Your accomplishments with families must be with students you are presently teaching, but your community accomplishments can be from the most current 5 years. If the school communities are quite diverse, you might want to mention both communities on the same form—just do so in a bit less detail. This is also a very good question to refer to the NBPTS hotline (1-800-22TEACH).

I've only been teaching for 4 years, so I haven't had a chance to be very active with professional organizations, committees, and the like. Consequently, my documented accomplishments entry is pretty short. Should I write about things that are less important in order to fill the page minimum?

Absolutely not! Restrict your accomplishments to those that have had a significant impact on student learning. You will not be scored on the length of your entries—only the significance of the content.

Is it a good idea to make a transcript of each of my videotapes?

Many NBCTs report that they transcribed every tape and used the scripts to identify significant exchanges. Others report that they viewed the tapes until they had just about memorized them. The procedure that works best for you will probably depend on your personal learning style.

If my entry is too long and it can't be pared down anymore, can I change the margins to make it fit within the required page limit?

This is not a good idea. Nor is it a good idea to use a smaller font size. In doing so you will risk that your entry will not be read—or that only a portion of it will be read. It's much better to edit the content of your entry to find places where your wording could be a bit more concise.

Do I need to hire an editor to look over my work?

Although some candidates choose this option, it is certainly not a requirement. Spelling and grammar will not be factored into your score. In fact, assessors receive a great deal of bias training prior to scoring that prevents them from considering the mechanics of your entry while they read it. That being said, it's a very good idea to ask someone who doesn't know you very well (or maybe even someone who's not a teacher) to read your entries. If they understand what you've said, you probably don't need an editor.

When packing the box do I need to send the release forms for each of my students and for the adults appearing on my videotapes?

No. You are required to keep the forms on file in your classroom or at your home.

Do I need to send the materials in the same box that the National Board used to send them to me?

Yes. If your box has been misplaced or accidentally destroyed, contact NBPTS at once.

What if I'm packing the box and I notice that the candidate number on my labels doesn't match the candidate number I've been assigned?

Hopefully you will have noticed this long before packing day, but if not, call NBPTS immediately to confirm your number and to inform them that you have someone else's labels. Then create labels of your own and attach them to the required forms and videotapes.

What's the best (and safest) way to send the materials to NBPTS?

If you are like most candidates, you'll be very hesitant to let your portfolio out of your control. You'll want to make sure it arrives . . . and that it arrives safely. Some candidates prefer to send their materials via insured mail, some use Federal Express, and others have been known to deliver it personally to the warehouse. Whatever method you choose, be sure to make at least one copy of your materials (written commentaries, student work, videotapes, and all forms) before sending the originals to NBPTS.

6

Preparing for the Content Knowledge Assessments

Adequate preparation for taking any assessment requires that you know what will be assessed. The National Board for Professional Teaching Standards (NBPTS) assessment process is designed to assess what a quality teacher knows and is able to do. When completing the portfolio entries, candidates demonstrate what they can do. The content assessment exercises determine what a candidate knows.

The assessment items represent the breadth of knowledge required of accomplished teachers in each certificate area. Because teachers typically specialize within their certificate area (i.e., candidates seeking MC Gen certification are qualified to teach ages 8–12, but most teach only one or two age groups within that range; secondary math teachers are certified to teach several different areas of content but typically specialize in only one), these exercises usually require candidates to brush up on aspects of their certification that they haven't practiced in quite some time.

Following is a list of things to get you started:

1. Print the assessment descriptions for your certification area from the Candidate Resource portion of the NBPTS Web site (http://www.nbpts.org).

2. Make a study notebook (or file box, or whatever you prefer) with one section in it for each assessment exercise.

3. Place a copy of the appropriate item description in each section.

4. Visit the Candidate Resource section of the NBPTS Web site again. Find (and complete) the assessment center tutorial. The tutorial will show you what the computer screens will look like, how to access your questions, and so on. It's *very* useful. There is even a simulated (timed) prompt for you to do (although it has nothing whatever to do with your questions!). Candidates quite often return to this section of the tutorial to practice speed writing with prompts that they think might actually be used.

UNPACKING THE PROMPTS

It's really not too difficult to anticipate the kinds of questions that could be on the assessment test. In fact, there are clues throughout the NBPTS Web site that can help you unpack each prompt and ultimately devise a plan for preparing yourself for the testing situation.

First, we'll unpack each prompt.

1. Copy the item description using a bold font.

2. Separate the sentences in the prompt, leaving space below each one.

3. Read each sentence one at a time and write down some thoughts about what the sentence means and what kinds of hints it provides about the question that will be asked on the assessment test.

4. Pretend that you are the test designer—write a question (or set of questions) that you think could be on the test.

5. Try to identify the universe of content that might be included in the item. For example, if an item mentions "science concepts," what science concepts are included in the curriculum for the entire range of ages covered by your certification area?

Following is an example of this process using the third item of the 2002–2003 EA/ELA assessment. After reviewing the sample, use the "Unpacking Prompt #__" form, identified as Resource 9, to unpack each of your content assessment items.

Sentences with comments:

Teachers will show their knowledge of the reading process and ability to analyze student reading.
I must show that I understand how students learn to read and I need to be able to determine where a middle school student is along that continuum.

> **They will be asked to read a passage, a student prompt, and a student response and to determine the reasons for misconceptions in the reading.** *I'll be given a sample reading assignment and a description of the student's response. I'll be asked to identify problems that student is having (i.e., misconceptions).*
>
> **They will also provide strategies to correct the misconceptions.** *I'll be asked to create a plan to help this student overcome the problems I identified.*
>
> **Possible questions:**
>
> 1. What are some misconceptions you see in the student's response?
>
> 2. What is the evidence of these misconceptions?
>
> 3. What are some reasons the student misunderstood the passage?
>
> 4. What are some strategies you would use to correct these misconceptions?
>
> **Universe of content:**
>
> This item only addresses reading in early adolescent years.

The final step in unpacking the prompts is to compare your ideas to the scoring rubric for that assessment item. Visit the Candidate Resource Center portion of the NBPTS Web site again. Download the scoring guide for your certificate. The content knowledge assessment rubrics are located in the back of that document. Compare your question(s) with the information provided about how this prompt will be scored. Make any necessary additions or corrections to your analysis.

Important note: If you are a candidate for a certification area that is available for the first time in the year you are seeking certification, your scoring rubrics will not be found on the Web site. NBPTS publishes all rubrics after the first group of candidates has been assessed.

SELF-ASSESSMENT

Now that you've unpacked the prompts and written a set of possible questions for each one, it's time to determine what you already know (but might need to brush up on) and those things you haven't thought about in a long time (or maybe ever!). But before you can do that, it's a good idea to identify the types of things you think you'll need to know to answer each question.

Use the "Self Assessment" chart identified as Resource 10 of this book to help you assess your knowledge of the content included in each item by doing the following:

1. Revisit each of the questions you think might be asked.

2. Make a list of things you'll need to know in order to answer each of the questions.

3. List the things you already know and probably won't need to study further.

4. List the things you have studied before, but it's been a while (things you need to brush up on).

5. List things you may need to learn.

6. Repeat this process for each of the items included in your assessment.

A sample chart based on item 3 of the 2002–2003 EA ELA assessment follows.

Possible questions (revisited):

    a. What are some misconceptions you see in the student's response?
    b. What is the evidence of these misconceptions?
    c. What are some reasons the student misunderstood the passage?
    d. What are some strategies you would use to correct these misconceptions?

What I need to know to answer these questions:

    a. Common misconceptions in reading among early adolescents
    b. Behaviors that indicate each misconception
    c. Common causes for each misconception
    d. How to remediate each misconception

Chart 6.1

Things I Know Learn	Things I Need to Brush Up On	Things I Need to
Oral reading errors	What the comprehension errors mean	More misconceptions
Comprehension teaching strategies	Comprehension remediation strategies	
Kinds of comprehension errors students make	Comprehension strategies for emergent readers	

Additional comments: *Elementary teachers might be able to help me understand how the misconceptions develop in the first place.*

FINDING RESOURCES

You have unpacked the prompts and made a list of the things you will most likely need to know for each of them. You have also identified those bits of knowledge that you already know, those you need to brush up on, and those you need to learn. It's now time to identify the resources that will help you prepare for the assessment exercises.

Resources may include people, technology, Web sites, books, movies, libraries, journals, universities, college textbooks, Advanced Placement exam manuals, museums, or any other place where you can find answers to some of your questions. Because each candidate differs significantly in what he or she needs to learn, it's very difficult to provide a list of appropriate resources that covers each situation. It is possible, however, to develop a system that will lead you to the kinds of resources that will be most helpful to you.

You have already created a chart listing those things you need to brush up on and those things you may need to learn. It's now time to generate a list of resources for each item you've listed in your charts. As you do so, it's critical that you analyze each topic/concept separately. Although it's possible that you could use the same resources for each item listed, it's highly unlikely (the chemistry teacher down the hall might be a terrific resource for you when brushing up on the latest developments in chemistry, but that same teacher may not be the best choice for assisting you with methods of data analysis). Use the "Finding Resources" chart identified as Resource 11 of this book to generate a complete and specific list of resources that you might be able to tap when preparing for each assessment exercise.

ANTICIPATING QUESTIONS

Being able to anticipate potential questions requires one more very big step. Some of the questions will ask you to demonstrate your knowledge of the content by analyzing student work (like in the EA ELA sample prompt we've been studying). Others will require you to actually solve a problem in your content area (e.g., the 2002–2003 EA ELA candidates were required to analyze a poem). Resources and study plans will differ significantly for each of these formats.

For each prompt determine
- if you will be analyzing student work or generating your own solutions;
- if you will be given student work to analyze;
- in what format the work might be given to you;
- where you might find samples of student work like those you will be given;
- where you might find sample analyses of similar student work;
- if you will be required to solve a problem in your content area;
- what kinds of problems they might present;
- where you might find samples of similar problems;
- where you might find strategies for solving problems like them.

Now that you've analyzed each of the exercises and generated a list of resources to help you prepare for the examination, you're ready to start studying. Some candidates prefer to create sample prompts they think might be given and study from them. Others prefer to study right from the charts. Whatever you prefer, take your time, check out all of the options, tap all of your resources, and when you think you're just about ready for the examination, proceed to the next activity.

PRACTICE MAKES PERFECT!

Many candidates find it quite useful to practice a few exercises before taking the actual test. Doing so builds their confidence as they become more comfortable with the computer and better able to respond to items within severely restricted time limits. There are a few more things to do before you're ready to practice.

Create a bank of sample items. Items used to practice may come from a variety of sources.

1. There are sample items included in each of the Scoring Guides. These items are retired prompts (ones that were used in previous years).

2. You may have created a few anticipated prompts while you analyzed each of the item descriptions.

3. Other candidates you know may have generated a few prompts.

4. Some universities have established Web sites where you can practice items they have created. (Check the NBPTS Web site for the latest information about these.)

If you have not already done so, find/write a few sample prompts. Create a separate document for each one and save them on your computer desktop.

Review the computer format. You have already visited the NBPTS Web site and explored the tutorial. Now is a very good time to revisit that part of the Web site and reacquaint yourself with the format that will be used when you take the test.

Plan for writing under pressure. Perhaps one of the most difficult aspects of the assessment test is the need to respond fully within strict time limitations. You will be required to read and interpret the questions, formulate your thoughts, and write those thoughts all within a very short period of time. Talk about pressure! But relax. Here are a few tips that should help you write under pressure:

• Before you begin the test, write down a few ideas you'd like to remember. You will not have time to write notes during the test.
• Read all of the questions/prompts on each of the pages before beginning to answer any of them. This will help you budget your time while creating a mental outline of your responses.
• Budget your time wisely. Decide before the test how much time you will allow yourself to read the questions. Decide while reading the questions how much time you'll allow for each one. Stick to your plan!

- Consider using bulleted phrases or lists instead of complete sentences. You are not assessed on your writing ability—only on your knowledge of content.
- Use the clock. You will have the option to turn off the clock. Choosing to turn the clock off, however, may result in spending too much time on one part of the exercise and not finishing.

The final part of the NBPTS tutorial is a timed response to a generic prompt. An excellent way to practice for the test is to replace the generic prompt with one of your practice prompts. Not only will this allow you to test yourself against the clock, but you'll also become more comfortable with the computer format. So open the tutorial, proceed to the practice portion, find one of your sample prompts, and write. Repeat with additional sample prompts until you feel comfortable with the format, the content, and the time restrictions. When you're done, you'll be well prepared for the actual tests.

Sleep well before the test . . . and good luck!

FREQUENTLY ASKED QUESTIONS

I'm not very comfortable speed-writing on a computer. Can I write the test answers by hand?

No. Beginning with the 2003–2004 cycle only a very few certificates allow handwritten answers (math, for example, allows you to solve problems by hand). Check the Candidate Resource section of the NBPTS Web site to see if your certificate area allows handwritten responses.

Where can I find resources that will help me study for these test items?

Each certificate area will be different, but a few general resources include professional organization Web sites and journals, college texts, publisher Web sites, teacher manuals of textbook series, museum Web sites (e.g., Smithsonian), state curriculum frameworks available on the Web (California has a great site), and advanced placement exams used in the high schools.

I'm not a quick reader/thinker. Can I possibly answer the questions in the time limit?

Yes, but you'll need to be very prepared and quite familiar with the computer screen that you'll be using. One of the best time-saving tactics is to scroll all the way through the first screen immediately—maybe even before you read it. It is not until you scroll through that screen that the actual questions will be shown to you. Reading the questions before you read the standards will help you "read with a purpose." Other techniques for saving time can be found on the NBPTS Web site. The questions are designed to determine the depth and breadth of your knowledge (i.e., how much you know without having to think too hard). Careful completion of the charts previously mentioned in this chapter will help you anticipate the questions and be prepared.

Part IV

Returning Home

Congratulations! If you are reading this page, you have completed your itinerary and are heading home. You have written and submitted all of the required portfolio entries and you have taken the content knowledge assessment tests. You are now looking forward to reintroducing yourself to your family and friends, to enjoying a full night's sleep, to eating proper meals, and to spending time away from the computer.

But wait! There are several more incredibly important stops on your journey: reflection, celebration, anticipation, and preparation. This section of the book is designed to help you reflect on your journey, celebrate your accomplishment, guide you through the scoring process, and help you prepare for your next professional destination.

7

Reflecting on Your Accomplishments

Y ou have just completed an incredibly powerful and revealing professional and personal development process. If you're like most candidates, you have covered a great distance as you navigated the National Board Certification process, and you have made several sacrifices along the way. It's time now to sit back, relax, and consider the impact this journey has had upon you . . . and to congratulate yourself on your extraordinary accomplishment.

REFLECTION

You will recall that Core Proposition 4 identifies accomplished teachers as those who think systematically about their practice and learn from that experience. Throughout the past few months, as you thought about various parts of your practice, you justified your choices regarding curriculum, methods, and materials and reflected on the appropriateness of those choices. It's now time to reflect on the certification process itself.

Teachers are often tempted to put their portfolio and content assessment study guides on the shelf or in a drawer on the last day of their journey without reflecting upon the impact the entire experience has had on them. Some of those teachers have every intention of returning to the portfolio after they've had a chance to relax a bit, but very often, their schedules prevent them from doing so. Teachers who do not reflect on the process short-circuit their chances for maximum professional development. It's important to reflect on the National Board Certification process as a whole, and the best time to do so is while it's fresh in your mind.

Following is a list of questions designed to help you reflect on your journey. Use the questions to trigger memories and/or draw conclusions about ways the National Board Certification process affected your professional growth.

What did you learn from the experience about

- your teaching?
- your students?
- the curriculum?
- yourself?

In what way(s) are you different for having completed the process?

- In what way(s) are you the same?
- How did your experience impact the learning of your students? Of their families?
- Are you glad you did it? Why?
- Would you recommend this process to a colleague? A friend? Why?

Now that you've reflected on the process, write a letter to yourself in which you reflect on the entire National Board Certification journey. Place the letter in a sealed envelope addressed to yourself and put it either inside this book or with a copy of your portfolio. Just prior to receiving your scores, retrieve and read your letter. Doing so will remind you of the power of the experience . . . and help put the scores into the proper perspective.

CELEBRATION

Completing the entire process is an accomplishment worth celebrating. A fairly large percent of candidates withdraw before completion, but you did not! You persevered through some fairly rough waters and reached your destination not only intact, but most likely as a stronger professional than you were when you began your journey. Do not take this accomplishment lightly. You have completed an enormous task. Celebrate your accomplishment! Celebrate your students! Celebrate your support system!

Celebrate Yourself!

You will find a Certificate of Accomplishment on the following page. Write your name (or the name of your class) on the line and hang it proudly in your classroom for all to see. Be proud of your significant accomplishment!

ANTICIPATION

Completion of the portfolio and assessments marks the beginning of one of the most critical phases of the National Board Certification journey—the waiting period. During this phase you will experience emotional highs and lows, feelings of

Certificate Of Accomplishment

is hereby granted to:

_____

for Completing all parts of the

National Board Certification Process

Martha H. Hopkins
_____
Martha H. Hopkins, MC Gen 99

great pride, and times of insecurity. Sometimes you'll think back on your work, confident that you wrote the most outstanding entries on the planet, and at other times you'll be sure that you totally missed the boat.

During this phase you may also experience a growing concern about how you should act when you achieve certification (or don't). You may begin to worry about the perception others will have about you as a teacher if you don't certify (or if you do). The uncertainty that marks this phase is best conquered with accurate information about scoring, knowledge of your options when your scores arrive, and a good support system.

SCORING

The National Board for Professional Teaching Standards (NBPTS) Web site (http://www.nbpts.org) includes an excellent discussion of the scoring procedures and criteria for achieving National Board Certified Teacher (NBCT) status. You should also receive complete directions for interpreting your scores when you receive them in the mail. Highlights of scoring at the time of this writing include the following:

- Each of the 10 assessments receives a separate score.
- If you score at or above 2.75 on any assessment, you will be considered accomplished in that area. Scores below 2.75 do not meet the standard of accomplishment.
- A total scaled score of 275 or higher is needed to achieve NBCT status.
- Each of the assessments is weighted, with the first three portfolio entries weighted the highest, followed by the Documented Accomplishments entry and, finally, the assessment center exercises.
- You do not need to achieve a 2.75 or higher on every assessment in order to achieve certification, but all 10 assessments must be submitted and scored in order to qualify

Perhaps the best way to clarify these criteria is to consider a few scenarios:

1. I ran out of time and only submitted 3 of the portfolio entries. If I score 3.5 or higher on all 9 of the assessments that I completed, my scaled score would exceed 275. Will I achieve NBCT status?

No. No matter how high your scores are, if you do not submit all 10 assessments you cannot achieve NBCT status. In fact, at this point in time, if you do not have a complete portfolio, you are not considered to be a viable candidate.

2. Suppose I get a 1.5 on one of my entries. Can I still achieve NBCT status?

Yes . . . but be careful here. When taken together, all of your scores must average 2.75. That means that for each low score, you'd need a high one to offset it. Mathematically, it's not as simple as it would seem, however, because of the weightings. That is to say, a score of 1.5 on one of the classroom-based portfolio entries is harder to offset than a score of 1.5 on the Documented Accomplishment entry.

3. Suppose my total score is 276, and my friend scores a 325. Is she a better teacher than I am?

Avoid comparing scores at all costs! When you become an NBCT, it means that you have met all criteria necessary to identify you as highly accomplished. Celebrate that and move on.

KNOWING YOUR OPTIONS

Perhaps the most important message in this book is that *you cannot pass or fail the National Boards*. If you do not achieve NBCT status on your first try, it does *not* mean that you are a bad teacher, or that you should find a different line of work. It also doesn't mean that the assessments are skewed or biased. What it might mean is that for some reason you were unable to paint an accurate picture of your teaching with the words you used. Or it might mean that you neglected to answer all of the questions or that there were some standards that weren't addressed completely in your work or that you are still developing as a teacher.

You'll recall that when the Five Core Propositions were written in 1989, they defined accomplished teaching and provided a structure and direction for systematic professional development. That is to say, they served as a vehicle for teaching teachers about teaching. When we teach students, we don't expect them to achieve mastery of content on their first attempt. Instead we provide them with multiple learning opportunities. Similarly, the National Board has designed the certification process to extend over a maximum of 3 years.

Let's suppose that you receive your scores after your initial submission and find that the total is less than 275. As you review your scores, you'll probably find that that some scores exceed 2.75 and some fall below. In an effort to encourage you to continue to pursue National Board Certification, NBPTS will allow you to redo any of the assessments with a score below 2.75. You may redo as many or as few entries as you think you need to in order to achieve the target score of 275, but you may only redo nonachieving entries. As soon as you apply to redo an assessment, your original score for that assessment will be wiped from the records (but all others will remain in the "bank"). When you submit the new work, it will be double scored. That is to say that two assessors will score your work and your new score will be the average of the two scores. It is important to mention that your new score becomes part of your total, even if it is lower than the original (although that usually doesn't happen). If, after the second submission, you still have a score below 275, you may repeat the retake process one more time.

Choosing to bank is often a difficult decision. Think about how much time and effort you already dedicated to this goal. Do you want to do it again? Obviously, only you can make that decision if the need arises. It is important to note, however, that many (if not most) NBCTs who banked at least once report that they learned more about themselves as teachers when they redid several entries than they had learned the first time around. Always remember that the process is a powerful staff development tool. The more you teach to the standards, the more accomplished you will become.

GATHERING SUPPORT

Perhaps the most difficult part of the waiting period is the length of time that elapses between submitting your work and receiving your scores. At the present time, the waiting period can be as long as 7 months. At first, you'll probably feel relieved that you're finished and not even think about it. But if you're like most candidates, as the notification date draws near, you'll begin to ask a series of "What if" questions (What if I don't certify? What if I do certify? What if I certify but my best friend doesn't? etc.). It's a very good idea to consider each of these questions carefully before you receive your scores . . . and to gather a support system to help you decide how to deal with each one. By anticipating all possible scenarios you can avoid much of the emotional roller coaster that accompanies this phase of the journey.

Following is a list of common concerns voiced by "candidates-in-waiting." As you read through the list, consider your own situation. Would the strategy(ies) listed work for you? What other strategy(ies) might be more effective?

What if I certify?

Will I be expected to do more at school?

What if the principal makes a big deal about me and causes professional jealousy among my colleagues?

What if my principal ignores it altogether?

Possible strategy: Talk with your school administrator(s) before scores are released; talk with the colleagues on your team.

There are five candidates at my school. What if I'm the only one that certifies? What if I'm the only one who doesn't certify?

Possible strategy: Some candidates choose to meet as a group to decide how they will communicate on the day the scores are released. Some candidates have chosen to come to school early on the day scores are released and access them as a team. Some choose to check the scores privately, but agree to tell each other before a certain time of day.

Will other teachers think I think I'm better than they are?

What if my colleagues are resentful?

Possible strategy: Meet with a trusted colleague to explore possible behaviors to avoid. For example, will your faculty take offense if you wear clothing with "NBCT" embroidered on it?

How can I celebrate my success without causing resentment or jealousy?

Possible strategy: Meet with as many colleagues as possible and make plans for how to celebrate. If they are involved with the planning, they will be more likely to embrace your achievement than to resent it.

What if I don't certify?

Will the parents think less of me?

Possible strategy: Most parents/families of your present students won't know you did this unless you tell them! If you tell them, let them know how difficult the process is. Show them your certificate of accomplishment.

Where will I find help in deciding if I want to bank?

Possible strategy: Talk with a previous banker. Also the NBPTS Web site contains a detailed description of how to determine which entries to bank—and a program that will even do the mathematics for you.

Will my colleagues and principal think less of me?

Possible strategy: The best is to involve them in the process while doing it. If you didn't do that, help them understand how involved the process is. Most principals and colleagues will be in awe of what you've already accomplished.

What if I don't achieve after I've banked?

Possible strategy: Talk with a two-time banker. Join one of the electronic groups; seek out a mentor.

What other questions do you have? What strategy(ies) might help you avoid or remedy the problem?

YOUR NEXT DESTINATION

What does it mean to be an NBCT? Does it mean that you are a better teacher than everyone else? No. Does it require that you do more at your school then everyone else? Not necessarily. Does it mean that you never have to go through the certification process again? No. What are the roles and responsibilities of NBCTs?

These and other questions are currently being explored on the NBPTS Web site and on several Web-based discussion groups. The NBPTS has recently instituted a renewal process that resembles a mini-portfolio demonstrating teaching excellence, student learning, and professional growth since originally achieving NBCT status. A common theme running throughout all of the communications is that an NBCT is first and foremost an accomplished teacher who positively impacts the learning of students while furthering education reform through teacher leadership activities.

So what is *your* next destination? Is it teacher leadership roles in curriculum, mentoring, or advocacy at local, state, and/or national levels? Is it renewal of your National Board Certification? Is it networking with other accomplished teachers throughout the United States? Is it action research showing the impact of National Board Certification on student learning?

Whatever your destination may be, remember to keep the students at the center of your activities and the standards ever present in your words and deeds, and the students of America will benefit from your expertise for many years to come.

Resources

Resource 1: Analyzing the Standards

Standard #_: _____

(Write the title of the standard here)

Evidence of This Standard in My Practice

Key Word or Phrase	What I Do	What I Could Do

Is there anything in your practice that seems to be contrary to the standard (i.e., you might want to change)?

_____

_____

_____

_____

Resource 2: What Am I Supposed to Do?

Entry Title: _____

Read the title. What are the key words? What clues does the title give you about content or emphasis of this entry? Write the title in your own words.

_____

_____

_____

_____

Italics. This abstract of the entire entry is found on the same page as the title. It is a summary of the scoring rubric for this entry. What clues does it offer you about what will be assessed in the entry?

_____

_____

_____

_____

Standards. Which standards are assessed in this entry? Reread the identified standards. Are there parts of each of these standards that seem more appropriate to this entry than others? Are there any standards that are assessed in this entry only?

_____

_____

_____

_____

Scoring rubric. This part describes how your response will be scored. What new information is presented here?

_____

_____

_____

_____

What do I need to do? What are the specific requirements about content, number of students, number of artifacts, and the like? List them here.

_____

_____

_____

_____

Questions (composing the commentary). Read and reflect on the questions you'll need to answer in this entry. What kinds of teaching experiences would help you answer these questions?

_____

_____

_____

_____

Making good choices. Now that you have a general idea about this entry, read this section to fine-tune your ideas. List your emerging choices here.

- Which students/class might be good to highlight? What challenge(s) do they present to your practice?

  _____

  _____

  _____

- What might be a good lesson/unit topic? How will that topic help you fulfill the requirements (i.e., demonstrate how you meet the standards)?

  _____

  _____

  _____

- When might be a good time to teach the lesson(s)?

  _____

  _____

  _____

- What will you be looking for when analyzing either the student work or your videotape?

_____

_____

_____

_____

- What other possibilities might you explore?

_____

_____

_____

_____

Resource 3: Videotape Options

Equipment used: _____ Videographer: _____

Camera placement:_____

Date: _____ Class period: _____

Quality of tape—good lighting?	
Are there any "breaks" in the tape?	
Can you see student faces?	
Do you hear student dialogue?	
Are student voices clear enough to understand their dialogue/discussion?	
Can you see your face?	
Can you hear your voice? Too loud?	
What about background noise? Too much?	
Does your room arrangement reflect a positive/safe learning environment?	
Camera movement too fast? Not fast enough?	
Can you see the materials you were using?	
Any surprises on the tape?	

Additional notes to yourself:

_____

_____

_____

_____

Resource 4: Writing an Accomplishment

Title: _____

What is the nature of the activity? [Detailed description]

_____

_____

_____

_____

How is the activity significant? [Beyond routine, impact, how addresses category(ies) and standards]

_____

_____

_____

_____

How has the activity impacted student learning? [Be specific.]

_____

_____

_____

_____

What documentation will you use for the activity? [How will you get it?]

_____

_____

_____

_____

Resource 5: The Main Idea

Entry: _____

Boldfaced heading: _____

Prompt	What I Must Do

Resource 6: What Does It Mean?

Entry: _____

Key Word or Phrase	Possible Definition

Resource 7: Finding Videotape Evidence

Entry: _____

Requirement	It Could Look Like . . .	It Could Sound Like . . .	Evidence on My Tape	Where?

Resource 8: Editing Checklist

Content

☐ Have you answered all of the questions thoroughly?

The Main Idea

Portfolio directions

☐ Does your entry show evidence of accomplished teaching?

Introduction to the entry (the italicized portion of the directions)

How Will My Response Be Scored?

Note-Taking Guide

Standards

☐ Is your entry tightly woven?

Logical

All decisions are based on evidence

☐ Is your entry in your own voice?

Would a colleague know it was your entry if he or she found it in the lounge?

Mechanics

☐ Is your entry easy to read?

Sentence structure/grammar

Spelling

Format

☐ Does your entry meet NBPTS requirements?

Font

Margins

Placement of candidate number

Page numbering

Total number of pages

Resource 9: Unpacking Prompt # _____

Sentences with comments:

_____

_____

_____

_____

Possible questions:

_____

_____

_____

_____

Universe of content:

_____

_____

_____

_____

Resource 10: Self-Assessment

Prompt #_____

Possible questions (revisited):

_____

_____

_____

_____

What I need to know to answer these questions:

_____

_____

_____

Things I Know	Things I Need to Brush Up On	Things I Need to Learn

Additional comments:

_____

_____

_____

_____

Resource 11: Finding Resources

Prompt # _____

Need to Brush Up On	Possible Resources	Need to Learn	Possible Resources

Index